Judging People

A guide to orthodox and unorthodox methods of assessment

Judging People

A guide to orthodox and unorthodox methods of assessment

edited by

D. Mackenzie Davey

and

Marjorie Harris

McGRAW-HILL Book Company (UK) Limited

London · New York · St Louis · San Francisco · Auckland · Bogotá
Guatemala · Hamburg · Johannesburg · Lisbon · Madrid · Mexico
Montreal · New Delhi · Panama · Paris · San Juan · São Paulo
Singapore · Sydney · Tokyo · Toronto

Published by
McGRAW-HILL Book Company (UK) Limited
MAIDENHEAD·BERKSHIRE·ENGLAND

British Library Cataloguing in Publication Data

Judging people: a guide to orthodox and
unorthodox methods of assessment.
1. Psychology, Industrial
2. Personnel management
I. Davey, MacKenzie   II. Harris, Marjorie
6583'001'9   HF 5548.8

ISBN 0-07-084581-6

Library of Congress Cataloging in Publication Data

Judging people.

Includes bibliographical references and index.
1. Psychology, Industrial – Addresses, essays, lectures. 2. Personality assessment –
Addresses, essays, lectures. 3. Assessment centers (Personnel managemen
procedure) – Addresses, essays, lectures.
I. Davey, D. Mackenzie (Douglas Mackenzie)
II. Harris, Marjorie (Evelyn Marjorie)
HF5548.8.J8   155.2'8   82-265

ISBN 0-07-084581-6   AACR2

12345 MCL 85432

Filmset in 'Monophoto' Times New Roman & Rockwell Light
by Eta Services (Typesetters) Ltd., Beccles, Suffolk
Printed and bound in Great Britain by Mackays of Chatham Ltd

Contents

Notes on the contributors

Editors

D. Mackenzie Davey, after qualifying as a psychologist, worked in research and then moved into personnel management, eventually becoming Vice-President (Industrial Relations) of the CVA Group. He then returned to a career in psychology and since about 1960 has been working as a consultant concerned essentially with the application of psychology to industry, including advisory work in the field of training, the conduct of attitude surveys, and, most particularly, the psychological assessment of executives. He lectures widely and has been co-author (with P. McDonnell) of *Programmed Instruction* (IPM, 1964); *Attitude Surveys in Industry* (IPM, 1970); *How to Interview* (BIM, 1975); and *How to be Interviewed* (BIM, 1980). He is an Associate of the British Psychological Society and a Fellow of the Institute of Personnel Management.

Marjorie Harris joined the Institute of Personnel Management as editor of the journal, *Personnel Management*. Later work included publications, development of the information service, publicity and press relations, creation of an IPM 'image', and conference planning. As Assistant Director (Services) until 1979, she was responsible for the IPM's income-earning functions: appointments service, courses and conferences, and publishing. Her major interest and activity was to set IPM up as a recognized publisher of management books, reports, and surveys. Her own contributions to IPM's list of books include *Married Women in Industry* and *How to Get a Job*. She is a Companion of the IPM, and in private life the Viscountess St Davids. She is currently writing and freelancing.

Contributors

Frank Welsh is an international banker and Lloyds underwriter. He has been chairman of steel, engineering, motor, and travel companies, member of the British Waterways Board and of the Royal Commission on the NHS. He has written a book on the nationalized industries to be published in the autumn of 1982.

Dr Sarah E. Hampson is Lecturer in Psychology at Birkbeck College, University of London. Her research includes studies of the personality of offenders and the perception of personality and emotions. She is the author of a recent book on personality, *The Construction of Personality: an Introduction* (Routledge & Kegan Paul, 1982).

Dr Clive Fletcher is Principal Lecturer in Psychology, Goldsmiths' College, University of London. A consultant on managerial assessment and performance, Dr Fletcher has extensive experience of assessment centres in both public and private sector organizations in the capacity of researcher as well as a practitioner. He has recently been involved in a major study of a UK-based assessment centre operated by Standard Telephones and Cables (STC) Ltd. He is a Fellow of the British Psychological Society.

Dr Mark Cook is in the Psychology Department of the University College of Swansea, University of Wales, and is working on a textbook of personality at graduate level, on a book of original material on the inheritance of intelligence, and on a book of contributed chapters on person perception. He is in the process of setting up a management consultancy in partnership with an ex-Swansea psychology graduate and a local insurance broker. One of its specialities, and his particular concern, will be the computerized administration and interpretation of personality, ability, aptitude, and interest tests, for selection, promotion, development, and vocational guidance.

Dr Rowan Bayne is a Senior Lecturer in Applied Psychology in the Department of Applied Social Sciences, North East London Polytechnic. His previous posts were with the Civil Service Department (research on selection) and Aberdeen University (research on self-disclosure). He has published widely on interviewing and related topics, e.g., self-awareness, and has worked as a consultant on interviewing for several organizations.

Dr Kate Loewenthal has held appointments in the Universities of London and Wales and City University. She has done outside consultancy work and has been involved in job and student selection and its methods. She has active research interests in the fields of social psychology, language and communication, cognition, and personality, and has published a number of articles including several on the relations between handwriting and personality.

Sheila MacCleod works for a major international computer company developing and teaching courses for users of information-processing systems. Since 1976, when she began teaching astrology at an adult education institute of the Inner London Education Authority, she has trained as a counsellor with the Centre for Transpersonal Psychology in London and now uses astrology as a counselling aid, particularly for people who need vocational guidance, help with a mid-life career crisis or support through a time of stress and change.

Dr David Nias is a research psychologist at the Institute of Psychiatry, University of London, and works as a consultant in market research and in personnel selection. In collaboration with Professor H. J. Eysenck, he has written a paperback book (*Sex, Violence and the Media*) which describes the evidence on the effects of pornography and violence on television.

Foreword

H. J. EYSENCK

Judging other people is one of the most important things we are called upon to do, and in some situations it may be a matter of life or death. Choosing the right person to be at your side in a battle; choosing your partner for life in marriage; choosing the right person to head important corporations, or the armed services, or MI5; or even choosing the right person to serve in an academic department, or a small business firm, or as outside right in a football club—these are more or less momentous decisions which, if you make a mistake, will have long-lasting and often severe consequences. No wonder men have for thousands of years invoked the help of the supernatural, have prayed for guidance, and have placed reliance on methods that are probably not very effective.

As an example, consider the story in the Bible in which Gideon is reported to have used a two-stage selection procedure in his war against the Midianites. As the first stage he used a kind of psychiatric screen based largely on reports of anxiety and depressive features. He had a proclamation read out to the effect that: 'Whosoever is fearful and afraid, let him return and depart early from Mount Gilead.' This seems to have eliminated two-thirds of the total, a more severe reduction in numbers than would be tolerated by most modern commanders.

However, Gideon went on to put into effect the second stage, consisting of a psychological performance test. This is described in the Bible as follows:

> And the Lord said unto Gideon, The people are yet too many; bring them down unto the water, and I will try them for thee there; and it shall be, that of whom I say unto thee, This shall go with thee, the same shall go with thee; and of whomsoever I say unto thee, This shall not go with thee, the same shall not go.
> So he brought down the people into the water: and the Lord said unto Gideon, Every one that lappeth of the water with his tongue, as a dog lappeth, him shalt thou set by himself; likewise every one that boweth down upon his head to drink.
> And the number of them that lapped, putting their hand to their mouth, were three hundred men: but all the rest of the people bowed down upon their knees to drink water.
> And the Lord said unto Gideon, By the three hundred men that lapped will I save you, and deliver the Midianites into thine hand: and let all the other people go every man unto his place.

However unorthodox, this selection procedure seems to have worked, because Gideon was in fact victorious. It is nevertheless doubtful whether a modern military commander would prefer such a test to those elaborated in selection boards during the Second World War.

The major difficulty in judging other people, of course, is that they usually know that they are being judged, and consequently are able to disguise those features in their temperament, character, and behaviour that are likely to lead to their rejection. Many a husband has found to his lasting unhappiness that the pretty, smiling, submissive girl he married turned out to be a sour-faced, tyrannical termagant, just as many a wife discovered that her attentive, gentle, and tender boyfriend after marriage turned into a sullen, philandering alcoholic.

In business, too, disappointments are frequent, and appointments made in haste may be repented at leisure. It is no wonder, therefore, that in recent years people have turned more and more to psychology to try and find better ways of judging people than those previously available. Methods of interviewing have been improved; psychological tests of intelligence and personality have been introduced; graphology and even astrology and palmistry have been employed by serious businessmen and personnel consultants in efforts to make the judging of people better, more objective, and more valid. Most interesting of all, it has been shown that different people have differential powers to judge others, some being very good at it, others very bad. Perhaps we can learn to apply the old saying, 'Quis custodes custodiet', in a novel way and rephrase it to read: 'Who shall select the selectors?'

An attempt is made here to set down what has been learned by experimental and applied psychologists about all these different methods, and thus to guide the prospective customer. There are as yet no perfect methods, but we can do somewhat better than chance or custom. The book outlines what is known; we have advanced a little way, even if most of the work is devoted to showing that methods favoured by many are in fact useless. This may not sound much of an advance, but it is important to slough off the dead wood before we can begin to raise flowers! And at least some of the modern psychological methods of testing have proved their usefulness, and may be relied upon to greater or lesser extent to improve on tradition: that too is an advance.

Introduction

D. MACKENZIE DAVEY and MARJORIE HARRIS

This book sets out to describe some of the more or less systematic ways that people use to judge others. Its purpose is to provide an appreciation of methods of judgement rather than a 'how to do it' manual or textbook. It is intended mainly for the man or woman in industry, commerce, public service, or the professions who is responsible for people as well as for money, machines, or services; and it should be of particular relevance to the personnel manager who is expected to assess others for new appointments or for promotions. Not least, there is also a readership among those of us who are judged from time to time when we apply for jobs, for places in higher education, and in other spheres where our characters, abilities, and potential are subjected to scrutiny: we need to know what we are up against.

There is, too, a widespread general interest in the subject; this is demonstrated by the number of articles in popular as well as learned journals and in many radio and television programmes. We have tried to meet this need for information by inviting some of our authors to discuss and explain the more usual methods, such as interviewing and other assessment techniques. We have also asked certain contributors to report their findings on less familiar approaches, which they have done with commendable honesty. In our experience, people *want* to know if 'there is anything in graphology/astrology/palmistry' as ways of assessing people: our authors give the state of play.

Man has always needed to judge his fellow man: at first, for self-preservation (does he form a threat?); later, for self-interest (can he help?); and still later, perhaps out of curiosity (how will he behave?). In efforts to answer this last question man has developed a number of different approaches to judging people. Many have roots in ancient history, and some, such as the techniques used by contemporary psychologists, are relatively recent developments.

From the descriptions of techniques, both conventional and unconventional, we hope that the reader may emerge with a reasonably rounded understanding of what is known about judging people; and if his curiosity is stimulated by a particular method and he wishes to pursue it further he will find that our authors have given references to other published works.

We have obviously not been able to cover all approaches. Some have been omitted because they have little relevance or value today; some because they have not yet been sufficiently developed; and some because we were unable to get contributions from experts. We regret that space has not allowed a description of certain selection procedures, such as the impressive programme for entry into the Civil Service in China 4000 years ago. We have not touched on the extraordinary boom in phrenology in the nineteenth century and the influence of Fowler,[1] who not only 'read heads', published books, arranged lectures, and established a museum of skulls and pictures, but also advocated temperance, vegetarianism, avant-garde architecture, shorthand, hydro-therapy, abolition of slavery, and equal rights for women: he was a marriage counsellor and a pioneer in the then forbidden area of sex education. But, while Fowler and his associates were campaigning so vigorously, others were conducting more rigorous examinations which have almost totally discredited the hypothesis underlying phrenology. The old phrenology 'heads', with their quaint descriptive terms, are now seen only in antique shops or, as a joke, in the studies of trendy psychologists.

Areas not discussed include the more recent work in body language, which is well documented elsewhere,[2,3] and one of the latest techniques, Kirlian photography, which has been the subject of some publicity. Since it is likely to be unfamiliar to some of our readers, a brief explanation of the approach may be helpful. It has been developed largely in the Soviet Union by Semion and Valentina Kirlian. Like many scientific discoveries, it began by chance. When holding a photographic film, Kirlian was exposed to a volley of electrical sparks; the images of the fingers and hand on the plate aroused the Kirlians' interest and they developed a high-frequency spark discharge in a controlled way. 'Photographs' taken by this method are claimed to be related to states of health and to differences in personality. Kirlian photography has now developed to a stage where it is reported that the body is surrounded by a field of brilliantly coloured moving lights—exactly like the aura claimed to be seen by clairvoyants. Contemporary advocates of Kirlian photography also link the method to palmistry because of the seeming unique individual differences of the photographs of people's hands.

Different methods of judging people range from the ancient—numerology, the cabala, tarot—to more recent techniques: the professional practice of graphology, electro-encephalography, psychoanalysis, scientology, colour choice, and the newer systems which explore the contours of the face, the size and form of the nose, mouth, ears, eyes, texture of the hair—back to physiognomy.

Our choice of techniques in this book is selective rather than comprehensive, but we had hoped to publish in addition some recent findings on intuitive judgement. Unfortunately, the complex analysis had not been completed at the time of going to press.

Although some of our authors provide links with other contributors to the text, each chapter is self-sufficient. There is therefore some minor overlapping, in particular in Chapters 3 and 4, which discuss an industrial psychologist's approach to assessment and assessment centres respectively. If these chapters are to stand on their own, occasional repetition of comments on psychological tests, for instance, are inevitable. In any case, we believe that the concepts of reliability and validity cannot be too strongly emphasized for the benefit of the non-professional reader.

The reader need not feel conscientiously obliged to work through the book from start to finish but can choose the chapters that appeal to him most.

After setting the scene by outlining the historical background, we thought it logical to begin with an examination of personality. In Chapter 2, Hampson argues that personality should be regarded not as a property possessed exclusively by individuals, but rather as something created as a result of individuals interacting with each other. 'It is through the social process that we construct the personalities of ourselves and others.'

In order to help us to contribute to our limited understanding of personality, we move from the better known methods of assessment to more unusual alternatives. Most people think that they know something about interviewing, and maybe about psychological testing and assessment too, and how these methods can be used to judge people. Mackenzie Davey, Fletcher, and Bayne deal fully with these topics (Chapters 3, 4, and 5).

Cook's valuable chapter (6) emphasizes that we should try to use valid information when judging others: information that has been shown by systematic research on a large number of people to predict what we want to know. He provides a useful lead in to Chapters 7–10, which venture into more speculative fields.

In her cautious chapter (7), Loewenthal asks whether it would be a good investment of effort to pay more attention to handwriting as a guide to the character and future behaviour of a person. She acknowledges that we are fascinated by the possibilities but holds that, at the same time, we are sceptical. Astrology in its various aspects also especially excites the popular imagination today. MacCleod's interest in applied astrology lies in its use as a method of self-judgement and personal growth (Chapter 8). Those curious about astrology should certainly read both Chapters 8 and 9, which are intended to balance each other. In his review of the practice of astrology and occupational success, Nias (Chapter 9) reports on a rigorous study carried out with Eysenck as well as on the work of other researchers.

The last of these potentially more controversial chapters is on palmistry, and we suggest that the reader should appreciate the care with which Bayne has made his comments (Chapter 10) in order to be fair while bending none of the rules of evidence.

The whole subject of judging people is in a state of continuous experiment and development. We hope the descriptions of a variety of approaches here will provide the reader with enjoyment as well as information.

References

1. Fowler, O. S. and Fowler, L. N., *Phrenology: A Practical Guide to Your Head*, Chelsea House Publishers, New York, 1969.
2. Morris, D., *Manwatching: A Field Guide to Human Behaviour*, Cape, London, 1977.
3. Lamb, Warren, *Body Code—The Meaning in Movement*, Routledge & Kegan Paul, London, 1979.

1. Judging people: The early background

FRANK WELSH

The influence of early art and literature

When we meet another person, our immediate reaction is governed by personal direct experience. If we have had one or two bad experiences with red-heads, we may be a little distrustful of that pigmentation; if our oldest and dearest friend is a tall Scot, we may start with a warm feeling towards long Scotsmen. But we are also, and less obviously, much influenced by the received opinions of our complex culture. Our perceptions and initial assessment of our fellows are conditioned and often confused by what art and literature has taught us to expect, and it is very difficult to dissociate ourselves from these preconceptions, which may often be traced far back. Our view of what the romantic hero should look like—eyes flashing, curls tossing, nostrils quivering, head at a defiant angle—dates from the representations of Alexander stylized by his court sculptor, Lysippas, and consistently followed by later artists. This is what heroes should look like, and people looking like this may be expected to be heroes. When, as often happens, heroes do not conveniently conform to such a pattern, popular imagination gives them a push in this direction. The short, fat, and lank-haired Napoleon is transformed by the painter David into something much more like the Alexandrian prototype; the tall and handsome Peter O'Toole takes the place of the short, undistinguished Lawrence of Arabia.

The Greeks: outward signs of personality

Our conception of how appearance reflects character begins indeed with the Greeks, who showed a lively interest in the outward signs of personality. Even Aristotle concerned himself not only with abstract ideas of what constituted just and virtuous behaviour, but on how this might be reflected in manners and appearance.

In the *Nicomachean Ethics* he reflects on how the proud and noble man (proper pride being regarded as a virtue, impossible without 'an ingrained

1

beauty of character') behaves in specific ways. 'He is severe with his fellows, but mild to his inferiors, scorning to use his moral strength.' There is nothing ignoble in showing one's dignity among the great, but to do so among the humble is like displaying physical strength against a cripple. 'He is generally truthful—it would be cowardly to lie—but may treat the *polloi* with light irony.'[1]

His character should be obvious in his outward appearance. 'The character of the proud man would seem to require that his gait should be slow, his voice low-pitched, and his diction measured.'[2] It is difficult to take this seriously—Aristotle's sense of the ridiculous was not ours—and his proud and noble man sounds like a pompous buffoon, and has served as a model for countless buffoons who wish to seem proud and noble. Malvolio echoes Aristotle 'and consequently sets down the manner how: a sad face, a reverend carriage, a slow tongue, in the habit of some Sir of note, and so forth':[3] as do a fair number of company chairmen, trade union leaders, and municipal dignitaries.

Aristotle's pupil Theophrastos (370 BC–287 BC), who succeeded him as head of the Peripatos, took things much further, with a good deal of wit and insight, into the analysis of personality. His 'characters' (the word *charaktēr* was employed to denote a type, rather than an individual; the later usage came in with the playwright Menander, Theophrastos' follower) were the first studies of personality types and are easily recognizable today. The Flatterer is by no means unknown in any large company: 'if you stop talking for a moment he puts in a "well said", and when you try some feeble joke he will burst out laughing ... at a dinner party he is the first to compliment you on the wine, with a comment like "what a connoisseur".'[4]

The Complaisant man is also still with us.

> At a dinner party he asks his host to have the children brought in, and when they make an appearance he calls them the very image of their father. ... He gets his hair cut all the time, too, and keeps his teeth painfully white. More than that, he changes his linen while it is still perfectly clean and he uses scented lotions. Downtown you can find him in the banking section.[5]

You still can!

Judaic standards of assessment

Theophrastos does not necessarily intend moral judgements to be made—he is an observer rather than a judge, although there is an implicit criticism of any conduct that deviates too far from an acceptable norm. Judaism, by contrast, was evolving standards of assessment in an uncompromisingly judicial fashion. Its judgements were based not on any descriptive analysis of the Theophrastan sort, but on a complex code of duty. Leviticus and Deuteronomy have 63 chapters between them, which lay down medical, dietary, sumptuary, sexual, and social regulations which must be followed. Judgement is therefore a simple matter of a check list: Garments fringed on all sides? Olive trees beaten only once? Good. Eating lobsters or herons? Bad! Force a girl in the city, and both must be stoned to death; in the fields, and she may go free.[6]

A code of conduct of such detail does not allow much for individuality: it is difficult and fascinating enough to attempt, as Rabbinical scholars have done ever since, to keep it up to date and re-interpreted. Although there are some indications in the Old Testament of an awareness that personality traits had outward expressions, these are dealt with cursorily: 'A naughty person, a wicked man, walketh with a froward mouth: he winketh with his eyes, he speaketh with his feet, he teacheth with his fingers.'[7] 'There is a wicked man that hangeth down his countenance, and making as if he heard not.' 'A man's attire, and excessive laughter, and gait shew what he is.'[8]

Chaucer's studies of character

The establishment of the Christian Empire was followed by the subordination of Greek to Jewish systems until after the twelfth-century Renaissance. By then, however, some other values had emerged, reflected in the highly individual portrait sketches given by Chaucer. These are both early and well developed studies of character. The Summoner, for example:

> That hadde a fyr-reed cherubynnes face,
> For saucefleem he was, with eyen narwe.
> As hoot he was and lecherous as a sparwe,
> With scalled browes blake and piled berd.
> . . . .
> And whan that he wel dronken hadde the wyn,
> Thanne wolde he speke no word but Latyn.[9]

And the Shipman:

> A Shipman was ther, wonynge fer by weste;
> For aught I woot, he was of Dertemouthe.
> He rood upon a rouncy, as he kouthe,
> In a gowne of faldyng to the knee.
> A daggere hangynge on a laas hadde he
> Aboute his nekke, under his arm adoune.
> The hoote somer hadde maad his hewe al broun;
> And certeinly he was a good felawe.
> Ful many a draughte of wyn had he ydrawe
> Fro Burdeux-ward, whil that the chapman sleep.
> Of nyce conscience took he no keep.
> If that he faught, and hadde the hyer hond,
> By water he sente hem hoom to every lond.
> But of his craft to rekene wel his tydes,
> His stremes, and his daungers hym bisides.
> His herberwe, and his moone, his lodemenage,
> There was noon switch for Hulle to Cartage.[10]

It is as easy for a painter to translate such descriptions graphically as it is for him to illustrate those of Theophrastos, but it is difficult for him to recreate any recognizable Old Testament character. Something of the Chaucerian values seem specifically northern European: the character of a saga hero is generally one of friendliness, co-operation, and sagacity, with the expected vigour and boldness in war and seafaring. He is also expected to have many of the virtues of a good drinking man: to hold his ale without becoming quarrelsome, to excel at the brag—an entertainment corresponding to a saloon bar story—and not be pompous in the wrong place.

Chaucerian descriptions combine physical with personality traits so powerfully and convincingly that they have become prototypes for posterity. The Shipman becomes the model for all subsequent mariners and pirates; we expect seafarers to be like this, and are somewhat aggrieved when they are not.

The humours

Among the rediscovered Greeks, the work of Hippocrates, the father of medicine, and his follower Galen, the second-century AD Greek physician, re-interpreted by medieval Arabian medical and philosophical writers, became increasingly influential. Chaucer knew the work of Galen, but it became better understood after the publication of the first printed edition in 1525. Among a good deal of sound medical sense—Laënnec discovered the idea of auscultation by reading Hippocrates—Galen taught the correspondence between macrocosm and microcosm. Man, like all creation, was compounded of the four elements, which the body received in its food, and converted in the liver to four liquid substances, the humours, which in turn corresponded to the original elements:

Element	Quality	Humour
Earth	Cold, dry	Melancholy (black bile)
Water	Cold, moist	Phlegm
Air	Hot, moist	Blood
Fire	Hot, dry	Choler (yellow bile)

Ideally, the humours should be balanced. Thomas Hobbes, who lived to be 93 and published his last book at the age of 87, was described thus by his friend John Aubrey: '. . . from 40, or better, he grew healthier, and then he had a fresh, ruddy, complexion. He was sanguineo-melancholicus; which the physiologers say is the most ingeniose complexion. He would say that there might be good wits of all cômplexions; but good-natured, impossible.'[11] Most men had a preponderance of one humour; Hobbes' father, who was forced to leave his benefice after 'a parson (which I think succeeded him at Westport) provoked him (a purpose) at the church doore, soe Hobs stroke him', is described, understandably, as a choleric man.[12]

Too great a preponderance of one humour produced not only mental but physical abnormalities. A surplus of the melancholic produced cancers, epilepsy, ulcers, paralysis, and depression; but at the same time there was a fascination with the melancholic. Aristotle (possibly) remarked that 'all those who have become eminent in philosophy or politics or poetry or art are clearly melancholics, and some of them to such an extent as to be affected by diseases caused by the black bile.'[13]

The Renaissance accepted the melancholic as the typical tragic hero, of which Hamlet is the archetype, and also as the dissatisfied, maladjusted, self-destructive malcontent, of which type Iago in *Othello* and Flamineo in *The White Devel* may be regarded as exemplars. The fashion was satirized by Ben Jonson in *Epicoene* (Morose cannot bear the slightest noise, a common neurosis: 'All discourses but mine own afflict me—they seem harsh, impertinent and irksome'[14]) and in *Every Man in his Humour* (Mathew is all agog to make acquaintance with Stephen, whose melancholy he takes to be an attribute of good breeding, for melancholy is the latest fashion):

> Mathew: But are you, indeed, sir, so given to it?
> Stephen: Ay, truly, sir, I am mightily given to melancholy.
> Mathew: Oh, it's your only fine humour, sir: your true melancholy breeds your perfect fine wit, sir. I am melancholy myself, divers times, sir, and then do I no more but take pen and paper, presently, and overflow you half a score, or a dozen of sonnets at a sitting.[15]

At least one sketch of the melancholy man approaches in depth a clinical study. The melancholy man

> is one that keeps the worst company in the world, that is his own. . . . His head is haunted, like a house, with evil spirits and apparitions, that terrify and fright him out of himself, till he stand empty and forsaken. His sleeps and his wakings are so much the same that he knows not how to distinguish them. . . . His brain is so cracked that he fancies himself to be glass, and is afraid that everything he comes near should break him in pieces. . . . After a long and mortal feud between his inward and outward man, they at length agree to meet without seconds and decide the quarrel.[16]

The melancholic could always be identified by his appearance, sallow, dark, etiolated, and languid, impossible to mistake for the sleek and ruddy sanguine, the flushed and rugose choleric, or the ponderous and dull phlegmatic.

The seventeenth century was fascinated by character types, and descriptive literature abounds: translations of Huarte's *The Examination of Men's Wits* and Levinius Lemnius's *The Touchstone of Complexions*, and John Earle's *Microcosmography* all produce sketches of corresponding psychological and physiological types, but in general make dull reading. They are often satirical, but rarely amusing; their authors are deservedly neglected literary figures. Much more lively are the authors who did not take psychology too seriously, especially la Bruyère in French and Ben Jonson in English. Jonson satirizes the preoccupation with humoural psychology in several plays, and particularly in *Every Man in His Humour* and *Every Man out of his Humour*:

> Cob: . . . what is that humour? Some rare thing, I'll warrant.
> Cash: Marry I'll tell you, Cob—it is a gentleman-like monster, bred in the special gallantry of our time, by affectation; and fed by folly.
> Cob: How, must it be fed?
> Cash: Oh ay, humour is nothing if it be not fed. Didst thou never hear that? It's a common phrase, 'feed my humour'.[17]

His own character descriptions are both funnier and richer, as in the Traveller: 'He doth learn to make strange sauces, to eat anchovies, maccaroni, bovoli, fagioli, and caviare, because he loves them.'[18]

In spite of physiologists and satirists, the theory of humours continued to serve as a convenient classification. There have indeed been modern attempts to test on a scientific basis the correspondence between humoural types and mental disorders. Ernst Kretschmer's *Körperbau und Charakte* in 1931 traced links between the body structure and mental disorders of depressives and schizophrenics, with some positive results. Inasmuch as depression is an experience of normality, except in its most severe forms, the literature of melancholia remains of more than antiquarian value. In the seventeenth century people were sufficiently attached to the humoural theories to be upset when science began to produce opposing evidence. William Harvey, whose evidence of the circulatory system cast doubt upon the physiological basis of the humours, regretted that 'after his booke of the Circulation of the Blood came out, that he fell mightily in his Practize, and that twas beleeved by the vulgar that he was crack-brained'.[19] But Harvey was an iconoclast by nature. 'He was wont to say that man was but a great mischievous Baboon . . . and did call the Neoteriques shitt-breeches.'[20]

The work of Lavater

The breakthrough in organized methods of assessment came in 1775 with the publication of Johann Caspar Lavater's enormous work, *Essays on Physiognomy* (*Physiognomische Fragmente zur Befordering der Menschenkentniss und Menschenliebe*). This enjoyed an immediate European success, being quickly translated into French, and thence into English: there were no less than 20 English editions in the 40 years after first publication. Of these, the 1789 edition translated by Dr Henry Hunter was magnificently illustrated, with more than 800 engravings, by the most distinguished artists of the day, including Fuseli and Blake, and formed an essential part of any gentleman's library. Fuseli was a friend and fellow countryman of Lavater's, and annotates some of the engravings with his own comments; Lavater reciprocated by including a physionomological study of Fuseli. This edition was called at the time the handsomest book ever published, and the illustrations combine with the text to give a striking exposition of Lavater's sometimes idiosyncratic views.

Lavater, a Protestant minister in Zurich, was a man of great charm and humanity, and a close friend of the young Goethe, who contributed to his work. Some, including Schiller and Schlegel, were sceptical, but many more were enthusiastic, and a visit to the accessible Lavater at Zurich became as much a part of the Grand Tour as had been the pilgrimages to Voltaire at Fernay and Rousseau at wherever he happened to be. Chateaubriand in particular was impressed, and his work reflects his enthusiasm: 'Toute l'antiquité a cru à la verité de cette science, et Lavater l'a portée de nos jours a une perfection inconnue.'[21]

Beginning by accepting the doctrine of humours, Lavater provides the usual sketches of exaggerated types. He goes further, in an interesting way, to analyse personality types by their reactions to events. One of his Fragments has representatives of the four humours admiring a picture of the *Death of Calas* and reacting, in posture and expression, in their different ways to the same stimulus.[22]

Physiognomy

Essays on Physiognomy is a diffuse and highly disorganized book, compounded of 'Fragments', 'Additions', and 'Notes', but it develops two themes strongly. One is the attempt to put phrenology on a scientific basis. The appeal of phrenology lay much in the fact that, before photography, accurate comparisons could be made only by measurement of the skull and the major features. For the same reason Lavater gives precise instructions on the making of silhouettes, a fashion that owed its rapid spread to the phrenological interest. Otherwise, the physiognomist had to work from pictures, generally engravings, rather than originals, and from live subjects. If pictures of great men did not coincide with Lavater's opinion of them, he had no hesitation in blaming the artist. He rejects the Gilbert Stuart painting of George Washington as historically inaccurate, since it did not follow the physiognomological requirements of a hero, and of a bust of Seneca remarks: 'This head cannot possibly be that of Seneca, if he is the author of the works which bear his name.'

Lavater, indeed, chooses his examples of military men, e.g., General Elliott, the hero of Gibraltar, and Washington, to suit his theories. It would be quite possible to refute them by picking even more eminent eighteenth-century soldiers, say, Prinz Eugen and General Wolfe, of very unmilitary appearance. It seems to be only some time towards the middle of the nineteenth century that military men felt themselves required to conform to a Lavater pattern; General Napier, the brilliant conqueror of Scinde in 1843, with his spectacles, shoulder-length hair, straggling moustache and umbrella, would have been absolutely unacceptable even 20 years later. It may even be possible that some of the excesses of military stupidity in the first half of the twentieth century were due to command being gained only by those who contrived to conform to received habits and appearance.

Lavater's phrenological work is ingenuous. He identifies character traits with animals, and traces similarities between animal characteristics and those of humans, exemplified in cranial similarities. This lent itself aptly to satire, such as that of Thomas Love Peacock's Mr Cranium:

> Every particular faculty of the mind has its corresponding organ in the brain. In proportion as any particular faculty or propensity acquires paramount activity in any individual, these organs develop themselves, and their development becomes externally obvious by corresponding lumps and bumps, exuberances and protuberances, on the osseous compages of the occiput and sinciput. . . .
> Here is the skull of a beaver, and that of Sir Christopher Wren. You observe, in both these specimens, the prodigious development of the organ of constructiveness.
> Here is the skull of a bullfinch, and that of an eminent fiddler. You may compare the organ of music.[23]

The features, as well as the bony structure, were classified by Lavater as individually denoting qualities: 'the nose [indicates] taste, sensibility and feeling; the lips, mildness and anger, love and hatred; the chin, the degree and species of sensuality'. Miniscule variations in the features are compared, often on dubious evidence, in such a way as to invite further satire and ridicule.

Other findings: body structure; body language

Much more significant and valuable was Lavater's insistence on the homogeneity of each individual. Every man will show his character in all that he appears to be and in all that he does—his features, his bodily structure, his hair, his voice, his language, his attitudes, his handwriting, and his dress, and all must reflect the same unity of character.

> Never can I, too often, too earnestly, repeat—combine the whole, compare each with each, examine the whole of nature, of form, the complexion, the bones, the muscles, the flexibility, inflexibility, motion, position, gait, voice, manners, actions, love, hatred, passions, weeping, laughing, humour, fancy, anger. . . . Neglect no single part; but again combine the single with the general.

Lavater concerns himself, too, with chiromancy and graphology, and makes the point that handwriting, although it can vary considerably according to the mood of the person, always contains a strong individuality, and cannot be mistaken readily for handwriting from a different individual. He also points out that strong national and local characteristics can be seen. He has two pages of handwriting examples, one of which is composed only of superscriptions of letters addressed to him. On this modest basis he makes an analysis of the character of his correspondents, which presumably was borne out by the contents of the letters. He quotes one previous writer with a note of approval that will be shared by most academics: 'Persons of superior understanding seldom write a fine hand.' Otherwise Lavater is critical of the work of earlier physiognomists, of which he prints a number of extracts summarized by the editor Henry Hunt in a note: 'The reveries of chiromancers and metapascopists, conveyed in obsolete French or still more barbarous Latin, is hardly possible to clothe in tolerable English or to reconcile with good sense.'

One feature the importance of which is much emphasized is the hair. Lavater reinforces one conception that has passed into the collective European conscious: that heroes, and perhaps more particularly heroines, must be blond. Lavater noted that 'in descriptive advertisements for malefactors you hardly ever find fair hair, but more frequently hair of a deep brown; sometimes likewise black hair with fair eyebrows.'

The study of what is now called 'body language' and non-verbal communication, which supplements for speech, was begun by Lavater.

> There is nothing more significant especially than the gestures which accompany the attitude and the gait. Natural or affected, hurried or slow, impassioned or cool, uniform or varied, grave or airy, free or constrained, easy or stiff, noble or mean,

haughty or humble, bold or timid, becoming or ridiculous, agreeable, graceful, imposing, threatening, the gesture is varied in a thousand ways. Learn to distinguish and catch all these shades and you will have advanced a step farther in the physiognomonical career and will have acquired a new mean to facilitate the study of man.

Lavater progresses from clinical study of idiots through exaggerated theatrical attitudes to normality. In one of these studies of exaggeration showing men in similar attitudes, legs apart and hands crossed behind the back, much in the manner of certain royal personages, Lavater observes:

Never will a modest and sensible man on any occasion whatever assume an attitude such as these—and if by chance his attention, strongly excited, should induce him to turn his face upward too, he will not however cross his arms behind his back; this attitude necessarily supposes affectation and ostentation. You may say of the personages of this vignette in general that they give themselves airs or in other words are conceited as a coxcomb.

In another study of how attitudes display character Lavater analyses a page from a Prussian drill manual and points out that it is easy to distinguish the ranks of men involved—not from their uniforms, but from the attitudes they are adopting. He notes that 'the military system carried especially to a degree of perfection which modern times present is the most complicated and profound which man ever invented for the management of his fellow creature'.

The work on body language culminates in these studies of normality, reproduced with Lavater's notes, which refer primarily to the attitudes and gestures.

According to my mode of seeing and feeling, I would thus explain these figures, which I have borrowed from Mr Engel's *Art of Mimicry* [Fig. 1.1].
1. The meditation of a man of the world, who directs all his skill, and all his powers of calculation, to one single point.
2. Is a very ordinary man, who has turned his attention to an object of small importance: in which, however, he interests himself to a greater or less degree.
3. Incapable of much reflection, this man directs a momentary attention to something that accidentally presents itself, and which slightly affects him.
4. The phlegmatic indifference of a character which never profoundly pursued an abstract speculation.
5. An indifferent, feeble, and even insipid character, though gentle and modest.
6. The irony of a cheat at the expense of his dupe.
7. The affected indifference of self-conceit.
8. The deliberation of one not formed for reflection.
9. Such a manner of listening can announce only a contemptuous character, joined to excessive presumption.
10. The disgusting grimace of an impertinent fool, who makes himself completely ridiculous.
11. The brutality of one of the lowest of mankind, preparing to give vent to vulgar rage.
12. The confusion of a poor wretch, without vigour of mind, and destitute of honour.
Note: Observe with what sagacity the Designer has assigned, to each of these subjects, a form of hat which may be called characteristic.

Figure 1.1   *Attitudes*

The following remarks refer to the attitudes pictured in Fig. 1.2.

1. The attitude of a man at prayer. If the look corresponds not with the demeanour, the Copyist is to be blamed. If I durst, without furnishing matter for laughter, I would add a remark, the truth of which will, undoubtedly, be felt by more than one Reader: a person with hair like this is incapable of so much fervour.
2. Childish desire, in all its vivacity. By transports of this sort, by emotions thus passionate, real desire is expressed.
3. The theatrical affectation of a man destitute of sense, and meaning to give himself airs.
4. The deportment of a Sage conversing with a Sage.
5. This extacy of love and respect does not announce an ordinary man.
6. It is thus we return on having lost something on meeting an unmerited denial, or on having fruitlessly employed the arts of persuasion.
7. I will not say that this Monk has the appearance of being afflicted at having missed a benefice—much less, however, can I say that his attitude is that of a good shepherd, deploring the straying of his flock.
8. This woman has the air of pursuing with her eye a beloved object who has just left her. It was, perhaps, her sister, or her friend—but I am certain it was not her lover.
9. The attitude of a man who is listening attentively. No one surely will ascribe to him either superior intelligence or excessive delicacy. He is a contemptuous character, and that is all.
10. This one has retired to reflect at his ease: he appears not to want understanding, but is rather unpolished.

Another aspect of non-verbal communication that interests Lavater is laughter.

I insist that the laugh is the touchstone of the judgment, of the qualities of the heart, of the energy of the character, therefore it expresses love or hatred, pride or humility, sincerity or falsehood—A physiognomy of laughter would be a most interesting elementary book for the knowledge of man.

This great collection of observations had an undeniable and direct effect upon the range and sensitivity of perception. The *Gentleman's Magazine* reported that 'His books . . . were thought as necessary in every family as even the Bible itself. A servant would, at one time, scarcely be hired till the descriptions and engravings of Lavater had been consulted, in careful comparison with the lines and feature of the young man's or woman's countenance.'[24] Captain FitzRoy, Commander of HMS *Beagle*, was concerned that, according to Lavater, Charles Darwin's nose portrayed a lack of 'sufficient energy and determination for the voyage'.[25]

Much more important, however, is the secondary effect of this increased sensitivity through the medium of fiction. At least one important case is well documented. Balzac was introduced to the works of Lavater in 1822 by Dr Nacquart, a devoted friend of Balzac who nursed him in his last illness. Nacquart had written a book which discussed the relationship between physiology and psychology, based on the work of Lavater and Gall. Balzac had Lavater's works handsomely bound, and 'For Balzac this became a sort of Bible.' Balzac himself noted:

ATTITUDES.

Figure 1.2 Attitudes

People of perception, diplomats and women who are the rare and fervent disciples of these two celebrated men [Lavater and Gall], have frequent occasion to note other outward indications of the workings of men's minds. Bodily habits, handwriting, tone of voice, manners, &c. have often enlightened the woman in love, the scheming diplomat, the astute administrator and the sovereign [Napoleon]—all those who need to know true from false. . . .[26]

Our cultural preconceptions

Although the direct influence of Lavater on Balzac was large (and not only on Balzac, for such unlikely figures as Baudelaire admitted to the same influence), the indirect effect on later novelists and dramatists, and even on later film and television writers, is incalculable. However little we may have been exposed to the prime sources, we cannot by now avoid viewing other people with a host of 'cultural' preconceptions. How far we isolate these in judging people is not clear, since there seems to be a strong element of simplification in this. Thomas Carlyle's father despised anyone shorter than himself, making height the sole measure of merit, and this may be a significant factor in many choices. The word 'tall' was used until recently as a synonym for 'bold' and 'manly', as still is the phrase 'walking tall'. Guardsmen and police are made artificially taller to add to their impressiveness. It has been suggested that the infliction of gout or ulcers is an indicator of ability.[27] It is certainly true that anyone who closely followed the Theophrastan model of the Complaisant Man would find himself a secure career still in most merchant banks, where he might find himself free from ulcers, if not from gout.

In spite of the development of modern recruiting techniques and the resources of modern testing methods to draw upon, these do not in fact seem to be much used in arriving at decisions as to the character of people. It is quite possible to test for as many as 15 separate qualities, even though reservations may be made as to the significance and accuracy of some of the assessment; but recent research indicates that only a very few criteria are used in arriving at decisions—rarely more than three and often only a single one.

The most exact job description to be found in literature must be that of Mr Jorrocks, when recruiting a huntsman for the Handley Cross Hounds:

> . . . a strong, active, bold, enterprising young man . . . must be desperately fond of hunting, and indefatigable in the pursuit of it . . . shrewd, sensible, good-tempered and sober; exact, civil and cleanly; a good horseman and a good groom; his voice must be strong, clear and musical; and his eye so quick, as to perceive which of his hounds carries the scent when all are running; and he must have so excellent an ear as always to distinguish the foremost hounds when he does not see them . . . be quiet, patient and without an atom of conceit.

Although there may be some tautology, Jorrocks specifies 19 personality traits, two physical skills, and two professional requirements. He conducts a long and thorough interview—six pages in all—but his decision is made on a single criterion; and James Pigg, although drunken, idle, slovenly, unintelligible, lecherous, self-opinionated, and having quite the size of boots to fit anyone else, is appointed because:

'Fond of huntin'? Oh faith is I—there's nout like huntin'.'
   'Dash my vig!, so say I,' exclaimed Mr Jorrocks, still brightening up, 'so say I!
it's the real Daffy's Elixir! The Cordial Balm of Gilead!'[28]

This is to do, as many of us recruiting have done: we prefer one indicator,
in Pigg's instance enthusiasm, to all those others we may have scientifically and
methodically enumerated, and there is not much evidence that we end up
better or worse satisfied. If researchers in pheromones are proved to be right, it
may well be that we base our preferences on even more ancient methods than
liking the look of someone; we really are drawn to them because they smell
good to us!

References

(The references given here are in the form of notes to sources, and differ from those of
succeeding chapters, which are mainly references to suggested further reading.)
 1. Aristotle, *Nicomachean Ethics*, IV, ii.
 2. Ibid.
 3. Shakespeare, *Twelfth Night*, III, iv.
 4. Theophrastos, *Characters* (Kolakeia), trans. Warren Anderson, Kent State
    University Press, 1970.
 5. Ibid. (Areskeia).
 6. Deuteronomy 22: 23–7.
 7. Proverbs 6: 12, 13.
 8. Ecclesiasticus 19: 30.
 9. Chaucer, *Canterbury Tales*, Prologue, 624–41.
10. Ibid., 389–404.
11. John Aubrey, *Aubrey's Brief Lives*, ed. Oliver Lawson Dick (1949); Penguin edn
    1972, p. 313.
12. Ibid., p. 306.
13. Aristotle (pseudo-Aristotle), *Problems*, XXXI.
14. Ben Jonson, *Epicoene*, II, i.
15. Ben Jonson, *Every Man in his Humour*, III, i.
16. Samuel Butler, *Remains*, vol. ii (1759).
17. Ben Jonson, *Every Man in his Humour*, III, ii.
18. Ben Jonson, *Cynthia's Revels*, Prologue.
19. John Aubrey, *Aubrey's Brief Lives*, pp. 289–90.
20. Ibid., p. 287.
21. Chateaubriand, *Essai sur les Revolutions 1798*, I, xviii (note).
22. John Caspar Lavater, *Essays on Physiognomy*, trans. Dr Henry Hunter (1789).
23. Thomas Love Peacock, *Headlong Hall*, ch. XII.
24. *Gentleman's Magazine*, vol. LXXI, p. 174 (February 1801).
25. Charles Darwin, *Autobiography*: published with *Life + Letters* (1887) and
    (complete) ed. G. de Beer, Oxford University Press, 1974, p. 41.
26. Andre Maurois, *Prometheus: The Life of Balzac*, trans. Norman Penny (1965), pp.
    103–4.
27. 'Gout affects more Rich than Poor, More Wise than Fools, and that Kings and
    Potentates, Generals of Armies and Admirals of Fleets, Philosophers and many
    others such as these are sufferers' (supplied by Stephen Redfarn).
28. R. S. Surtees, *Handley Cross*, vol. I, Ch. 17.

2. Constructing personality

SARAH E. HAMPSON

Despite the proliferation of personality theories and personality tests over the last 30 years, psychologists still disagree over what they mean by the term 'personality', and cannot measure it with any great precision. Hence, there is a place for a book such as this, in which alternatives to conventional personality assessment are described in addition to the standard techniques. Any contribution to our limited understanding of personality is welcome.

Although disagreement is endemic in the field of personality, there is one point on which all approaches, from the science of psychometrics to the art of palmistry, are in agreement. They all share the assumption that personality is something that each individual *possesses* and which may therefore be regarded as existing *within* individuals. It is my aim in this chapter to take a critical look at this key assumption. I shall be arguing that personality should be regarded not as a property possessed exclusively by individuals but rather as something created as a result of individuals interacting with each other. It is through the social process that we construct the personalities of ourselves and others.

Looking at personality in this new light is not a merely academic exercise. It helps us to understand why attempts in the past at theory and measurement have been so unsatisfactory, and suggests which directions might be more profitable for the future. In particular, it helps to give us insights into what we are doing when we attempt to judge others through personality assessment.

This chapter is organized in the following way. First, it looks more closely at the fundamental assumption behind the concept of personality. This assumption will then be challenged by presenting the idea that personality exists *between* individuals as well as *within* them. From this idea comes the view that personality is a construction composed of three building blocks: organic properties of the individual; the perception of the person by others; and the perception of that person by him or herself. Each of these building blocks will be described, and I shall attempt to show how they slot together to form personality. Finally, this constructivist view of personality will be related to conventional views by showing how, when experts assess personality, they are describing the end-product of the construction process.

Fundamental assumption or fundamental error?

The personality assumption

Personality is not a part of the human anatomy that may be cut out and dissected. Instead, it is an insubstantial entity which we strive to capture so that we may pin it down and inspect it. We do this because we believe that it will enable us to understand why people behave in the way they do and hopefully even to predict their future behaviour.

Personality is, therefore, an abstract concept or *hypothetical construct*; and, as such, it can never be measured directly but can only be inferred from overt signs. The signs that are used for inferring personality are many and varied. They range from physiological measures, such as the salivary response to lemon juice, through self-report personality questionnaires, to the pattern of lines on the palm of the hand or the manner in which a house is drawn. There is no logical reason for excluding any observable human characteristic as a potential indicator of an underlying personality dimension.

The assumption that personality is a property existing within individuals is concisely expressed in Child's definition, in which it is proposed that 'personality' refers to 'more or less stable, internal factors that make one person's behaviour consistent from one time to another, and different from the behaviour other people would manifest in comparable situations'.[1] From this point of view, it is the task of the personality expert to decide what these stable, internal personality factors are and to set about finding reliable ways of measuring them.

This view underlies both professional and lay personality assessors. For we are all personality experts in so far as we all form impressions of others' personalities and use these impressions to guide our interactions. When we operate as personality experts, we organize our knowledge of a person to form a personality impression which we typically convey via the language of personality description or *trait* language. For example, we may describe one friend as 'tough', 'honest', and 'reliable' and another as 'adventurous', 'witty', and 'energetic'. Personality traits refer not to directly observable characteristics of the person but to underlying dispositions which are assumed to give rise to these observable characteristics.

In sum, the fundamental assumption underlying the conventional concept of 'personality', used both by professionals and lay persons, is that 'personality' refers to qualities that exist within the individual which are responsible for stable and consistent behaviour. In my view,[2] the fundamental assumption underlying the conventional concept of personality is also a fundamental error.

The personality error

There is a branch of social psychology known as 'attribution theory' which is concerned with studying the explanations people give for their own and others' behaviour (see K. G. Shaver for a concise introduction to this topic[3]). When we explain a person's behaviour, our responses, or 'causal attributions', fall fairly clearly into one of two categories: we say either that a behaviour was caused by the internal disposition of the person, or that it was caused by external characteristics of the situation. We make *dispositional* or *situational* attributions. For example, if a person walks into the room and trips over the carpet we can explain that behaviour either in dispositional terms, and regard the person as inattentive and clumsy, or in situational terms, and decide that the carpet is dangerously fitted and causes accidents. When we describe a person with a trait we are explaining his or her behaviour by making a dispositional attribution.

There is a strong tendency for us to make more dispositional attributions than are warranted, and this bias on our part has been termed by psychologists[4] the 'fundamental attribution error'. We are eager to explain other people's behaviour by appealing to their internal dispositions such as intelligence or personality, and we are reluctant to see behaviour as being determined by situational forces. The assumption that personality is located solely within individuals is a further extension of this fundamental attribution error.

We are constantly bombarded with a mass of sensory information from the external world; psychologists[5] have long been aware that in order to make sense of all this input we have to organize it with the aid of mental categories that we impose on the undifferentiated mass of information available in the real world. Objects and behaviours exist in the real world, but they come to mean something to us when we categorize them. For example, the sight of a large bird flying past at great speed takes on new significance when we are informed by an excited ornithologist that it may be categorized as a stooping peregrine falcon. It is by viewing traits as categories that we see the error in assuming that personality exists solely within the individual. It is just as much a collection of categories in the mind of the observer imposed on that individual to make sense of his or her behaviour as it is a collection of dispositions that may be regarded as residing within the person and causing behaviour.

We use the language of personality description to summarize our knowledge of someone's social behaviour. Traits are categorizing concepts which provide a convenient shorthand for communication. Instead of saying that Jane gives money to charity, buys people drinks, and likes giving presents, we encapsulate all this information by saying 'Jane is generous'. Traits serve as categorizing concepts for interpersonal behaviour in much the same way that categories such as 'animal' and 'vegetable' are ways of categorizing certain objects in our world.

To point out that personality's fundamental assumption is also its fundamental error is not to deny the reality of personality. Identity develops as a result of transactions in the social world. When we judge people, we categorize their behaviour according to a set of personality categories. Thus we *construct* their personality from our perceptions of their behaviour and its social significance.

Personality has come about as a result of human beings living together in an interdependent social system. It has been constructed out of the building blocks of behaviour and the meanings ascribed to that behaviour by others. In addition, there is a third building block that must also be taken into account. In the same way that we can observe other people and impose personality categories on them, we can also observe ourselves. The ability to observe our own personalities is a product of our unique capacity for self-consciousness. In the next section, each of these contributions to the construction of personality, *the observed*, *the observer*, and *the self-observer*, will be presented in more detail.

The elements of personality construction

The observed

The repertoire of human behaviour is in part determined by the biological characteristics of the human species and in part shaped by social forces. A person's identity comes about as a result of the interplay between his or her physical self and society.[6] What biological predispositions does the individual bring to the building site of social life where personality is constructed?

Biological explanations of human behaviour make a distinction between species-specific characteristics, which are found in all human beings and distinguish us from other animal species, and characteristics on which individual members of the species vary, giving rise to individual differences within the species.[7] Biological explanations have become popular recently with the rise of sociobiology,[8] which gives us a view of personality as something essentially pre-programmed by heredity. Species-specific characteristics are said to include such complex psychological dispositions as altruism in addition to behaviour more generally recognized as being biologically based, such as eating. The socio-biological view is not incompatible with some current approaches to personality which one would not immediately associate with genetic factors. For example, existential personality theories such as Maslow's[9] assume that all human beings have an innate tendency towards self-actualization, and this could be regarded as a species-specific characteristic. The directed, or teleological, view of personality development is also present in the rationale underlying palmistry (see Bayne, Chapter 10 below).

The possibility that individual differences in personality have a genetic basis has been explored in particular by Eysenck.[10] He has postulated that a person's level of extraversion is the result of his or her characteristic level of cortical activity, which is believed to be mediated by a part of the brain stem called the reticular activating system. It is not surprising that a theory that assumes a close relation between biology and personality should advocate physiological indicators of personality traits. For example, in the lemon drop test,[11] introverts are supposed to produce more saliva than extraverts when a drop of lemon juice is placed on the tongue.

The principle that people are born with specific combinations of characteristics that will make them different from others underlies astrological theories of personality, in which it is believed that the particular position of the planets at the time of a person's birth will determine his or her unique personal qualities (see Chapter 9 below).

The biological characteristics of the individual form one element of personality construction, but they do not, in themselves, amount to personality. They may set limits on that individual's behaviour, but so does society.[12] It is through the creation of social behaviours with social significance that human beings come to see behaviour as having meaning and to use it to infer underlying personality dimensions.

The observer

In order to function as social beings we all have to be personality experts. Social psychologists have studied people's beliefs about personality, calling them 'implicit personality theories', and have found that, within English-speaking Western society, people's implicit personality theories are very similar.[13] These theories are dubbed 'implicit' because much of this knowledge is not available in the sense that we could write it all down. After all, there are nearly 18 000 trait words in our language, which gives rise to a vast number of permutations of trait combinations.

Implicit personality theories allow us to consider personality in two ways. First, we can organize our knowledge about the person in such a way as to produce a description of his or her personality. Although we often do this informally, such as when we describe one friend to another, the occasion when it becomes most apparent is in writing character references. Studies of written and spoken descriptions of others indicate that a wide range of information is regarded as relevant in a personality description.[14] In addition to using personality traits, factual information concerning the person's age, occupation, and even material possessions is often included.

The second use to which implicit personality theories are put is in making personality inferences. On the basis of relatively little information, we are able to make judgements about the presence or absence of other personality characteristics. For example, say a friend invites me to a party where I do not expect to know any of the fellow guests: on the basis of the thumbnail personality sketches given by this friend, I am able to infer further characteristics about the guests. Thus, on hearing that Mike is 'friendly' I decide to chat to him because I believe that friendly people tend to be sociable and talkative. When someone cuts his hand on a broken bottle I seek out Moira, because I have heard that she is 'sensible' and believe that sensible people are likely also to be practical and calm.

How far are these implicit personality theories accurate reflections of reality? In other words, are we good at personality description and do we make reasonable personality inferences? The demand for the tools of personality assessment, both more and less conventional ones, suggests that we are not too convinced of our abilities as lay personality theorists. There are two ways in which implicit personality theory could fail to represent reality. First, beliefs about trait relations could be inaccurate. I believe that people who are sensible are also likely to be practical, but perhaps I am bewitched by the similarity in meaning between the two words to the point that I erroneously believe that they will be found together in the same person.[15] But presumably erroneous beliefs would not be borne out by experience and would be subject to revision. If implicit personality theories were so riddled with errors, they would not work as well as they do.

The other sense in which implicit personality theories could be wrong lies in their accuracy for judging particular individuals. While I may be right in believing that most sensible people are also practical, how can I be sure that, for example, Moira, who I believe to be sensible, is not an exception to the general rule and is one of those people who is not practical? I could project my beliefs on to her and be disappointed when she fainted at the sight of blood. There is a high price to be paid for misjudging people, and therefore we wish to confirm subjective assessments with more objective techniques.

As Mark Cook has shown (see Chapter 6 below), we do make errors when we judge others' personalities, and this is because we make mistakes in applying implicit personality theories.[16] People tend to underestimate just how limited a sample of a person's behaviour they are exposed to. We can probably all recollect occasions when we were surprised at the difference in a person we thought we knew quite well when seeing him or her in a new context. Knowledge of a person derived from a narrow range of situations is liable to be misleading, since situations usually limit the range of behaviours a person may perform. This is why selection procedures sometimes include more informal social situations in addition to the interview as a way of obtaining wider knowledge of the candidates.

Another consequence of being exposed to only a limited sample of a person's behaviour is that we are tempted to make the fundamental attribution error and assume that his or her behaviour in that situation is the result of personality dispositions and not simply due to situational factors. It is then assumed that these personality dispositions will cause the person to behave similarly in different situations, and we are surprised when this does not happen.

When considering the question of whether implicit personality theories are accurate reflections of reality an insurmountable problem is encountered. There is no genuinely objective criterion against which to compare implicit beliefs because personality can never be directly observed but must always be inferred. One solution might be to compare implicit personality theories with formal personality theories such as Eysenck's or Cattell's, which have been derived from extensive scientific investigation.

Such comparisons, while interesting, are misleading. It is impossible for even the most rigorous of scientific researchers to avoid the subjective element of personality. Careful scrutiny of both Eysenck's and Cattell's personality theories reveals that they were both founded, in effect, on implicit personality theory and not on purely objective observations. Eysenck chose to investigate extraversion–introversion and neuroticism–stability as a result of his extensive reading, both ancient and modern, of people's beliefs about personality.[17] Cattell[18] began his investigations by reducing the 18 000 trait words to a more manageable 35 scales covering distinct aspects of personality. Both investigators' initial studies, which formed the basis of all their subsequent work, involved having people rate other people on personality scales, and were therefore as much studies of the observers' beliefs about personality as they were studies of the personalities of those being observed.

The impossibility of achieving a truly objective personality theory devoid of bias from implicit personality theories results from the fact that personality exists as much in the mind of the observer as it does in the observed. By accepting that personality is a construction, the absence of an objective criterion need no longer be regarded as a problem. The observer imposes trait categories on to observed behaviour and constructs a personality for the person under observation. Sometimes, as we have seen above, this construction proves unreliable because of the over-zealous application of implicit personality theory.

The self-observer

Human beings are probably unique in possessing a highly developed degree of self-awareness. This means that we can observe ourselves in much the same way that we observe other people. When we think about our own personality we can apply our implicit personality theories to ourselves as readily as we can to others. We obtain information about our personalities from three sources, each of which will be described in turn: private information, other people's views of us, and public information.

Private information. We have privileged access to our private thoughts, feelings, and past experience, but there is a danger in placing too much emphasis on the value of this information. We often use it when we try to explain our behaviour, but frequently these explanations are wrong.[19] This point was demonstrated in a study of insomniacs by Storms and Nisbett.[20]

Most insomniacs attribute their sleeplessness to the stresses and strains in their daily lives, and Storms and Nisbett hypothesized that, if insomniacs could be led to change their explanations for their sleeplessness, they would be able to overcome their insomnia. Storms and Nisbett succeeded in helping one group of insomniacs to get to sleep 28 per cent faster than normal by giving them a pill which they were told would produce all the classic symptoms of insomnia (e.g., mental alertness and physical discomfort). Another group of insomniacs took 42 per cent longer than normal to get to sleep when they had been given a pill they were told would reduce the symptoms of insomnia. The pills in both cases were actually ineffectual placebos, and a control group who received the pills, but no explanation of their effects, reported no change in sleeping patterns.

Storms and Nisbett believed that the descriptions of the pills' effects would cause the insomniacs to change their explanations of their symptoms: the first group could blame them on the the pills, and hence sleep better, whereas the second group would sleep worse, since their symptoms had proved so unresponsive to the pills. However, when the insomniacs were asked for their own explanations of the changes in their sleeping patterns, they did not refer to the pills and their effects. Instead, the first group explained their improvements in terms of the good things that had happened to them that day and the second group blamed their bad nights on the bad things that had happened to them. When the experimenters pointed out the connection between the pills and sleeping patterns, the insomniacs politely dismissed it as an interesting theory but certainly not true for them!

Experiments such as these caution us against placing too much faith in our explanations of our behaviour. Since personality is often invoked as an explanation for behaviour, we must think twice before believing ourselves when we say 'I did that because I am impulsive' or 'I refrained from that because I am sensible'. Maybe the real control over what we did lay in some situational variable and not in us at all.

Other people's views of us.   In order to understand our own personalities we need to have an idea of the views other people have of us. Thus, if I think I am, say, a cautious person I can check on this self-observation by trying to figure out whether other people see me as cautious, too.

The importance of being able to see ourselves as others see us was stressed by a group of social psychologists known as symbolic interactionists. They did not test their ideas empirically but others have done so subsequently.[21] From these studies it may be concluded that, although the way we see ourselves corresponds with our perceptions of the way others see us, we are not so good at perceiving how things really are. Our self-perceptions differ considerably from the way other people actually see us, and the way we think other people see us also differs from how they actually see us. So again, in this second source of information about ourselves, there is plenty of scope for error.

Public information.   The third source of information about ourselves is probably the least erroneous. In addition to observing the private aspects of ourselves, we can also observe our public behaviour in much the same way as someone else might do. We can then make inferences about ourselves on the basis of these self-observations. Our knowledge of our public behaviour is probably more complete than an observer's could be. After all, we see ourselves in every situation and not just a limited sample, and hence have a unique advantage here.

Our self-observations can never be as complete as we would like since we can never fully step outside ourselves to get a three-dimensional self-view. Perhaps this is why we are so fascinated by astrological forecasts and fortune-tellers as well as by personality questionnaires and psychotherapy. We are aware that our self-knowledge is imperfect and are intrigued by the insights that other sources can offer (see the discussion of the Barnum effect in

Chapters 10 and 6 below by Bayne and Cook). Inaccurate and incomplete as our self-knowledge is, it nevertheless is important in the construction of personality. In particular, the significance of our wide knowledge of our public behaviour for the assessment of personality has been demonstrated in recent studies.

Self-observations have proved crucial in resolving contradictions between different measures of the same personality traits. For example, Bem and Allen[22] obtained self-ratings, self-report questionnaires, parental and peer ratings for the traits of friendliness and conscientiousness. Initially, it was found that these measures did not agree strongly with one another. Bem and Allen asked the subjects to assess how much they perceived themselves as varying from one situation to another on these traits and then divided them into two groups of high variability and low variability. When the different measures of the two traits were reconsidered for these two groups separately, it was found that there was very strong agreement between the different measures for low variability subjects and poor agreement for the high variability subjects.

Bem and Allen's study suggested that not all traits are equally relevant for all people. Relevant traits are ones on which people regard themselves as being relatively invariant from situation to situation, and it is only measures of these traits that will be reliable and of predictive value. Self-observations of variability have been used successfully in at least two studies since Bem and Allen's.[23,24] They seem to be particularly appropriate for traits that subjects perceive as more publicly observable, presumably because self-knowledge is most accurate for these traits.

The consequences of self-knowledge for personality

Personality experts tend to underestimate the extent to which people decide what sort of personalities they wish to project and set out to behave accordingly. In contrast, this assumption underlies much of the psychology of behaviour change and social skills training in particular. Here, the client is educated about the effects of his or her behaviour on others and is shown how to improve them.

Stressing the role of self-awareness in personality construction gives the impression that much of an individual's personality could be regarded as a pose or an act. Where, one might ask, is the *real* person? How can we cut through the superficial and contrived impression and reach the authentic underlying personality? I do not subscribe to the view that deliberate impression management should not be regarded as personality. The sociologist Erving Goffman has long been arguing that personality consists of the sum total of an individual's social roles,[25] and that society provides a range of settings in which these roles are played out. Thus, a woman may be a business executive at work, a mother at home with her children, and a daughter on a visit to her parents. In each setting she is playing a role—some more consciously than others, but they all add up to her personality and no one role is less authentic than any other.

The job interview is a classic example of a situation calling for a highly specialized form of role play; and yet, if the interview panel have reason to suspect that the candidate is 'putting on an act', they will regard him or her in a very poor light. This point was demonstrated in an experiment by Jones, Davis, and Gergen.[26] Subjects saw videotapes of two fictitious job interviews. The candidates were being interviewed either for a job as an astronaut or for a job as a submariner. Either they said things about themselves that were congruent with the astronaut role (i.e., being able to function effectively in isolation), or they said things that were congruent with the submariner role (i.e., being able to get along with others). The experimenters were interested to see if the subjects would form different impressions depending on the congruency between the candidates' role behaviour and the job for which they were being interviewed. Subjects were asked to rate the candidate on a series of personality scales after watching each film. It was found that the subjects were more confident to rate candidates who had behaved out-of-role than in-role; they regarded out-of-role behaviour as more informative than in-role behaviour.

This experiment implies that there is a Catch 22 inherent in the job interview. If the candidates behave in role-appropriate fashion we tend to be distrustful, but if they behave out-of-role we would not select them for the job. The way out is for the personality expert to stop being so distrustful of role-playing and appreciate that it is an integral part of social life.

In summary, in order to understand personality, human beings' unique capacity to be self-observers cannot be ignored. Although self-observations may sometimes be inaccurate, they do contribute to the construction of personality. Personality assessment has proved to be more accurate for traits that the subjects themselves regard as being a consistent aspect of their publicly observable personalities. The capacity for self-awareness allows us to attempt to perceive ourselves as we think others see us. As a result, we are able to manipulate the impressions we create. Different situations call for different facets of personality and effective social life requires a certain amount of deliberate impression management. When personality is constructed between individuals, the individuals are not only observing each other: they are also observing themselves.

Assessing constructed personality

In this chapter three contributions to personality have been proposed. First the characteristics of the individual that are primarily inherited and relatively independent of cultural influences were discussed. While all psychology can be reduced to biology, it is not always helpful to do so, and personality is so much an interpersonal product that just considering the organism's biological potential alone is inadequate. The second contribution comes from the consideration of the interpersonal aspect of personality, focusing on the role of other people as observers of personality. People observe behaviour and impose meaning and social significance upon it. They then infer that this socially significant behaviour is indicative of underlying personality dispositions. It is in the combination of the contribution of the biological component, which creates the potential for certain sorts of behaviour, plus the social/cultural component, in which people impose meaning on behaviour, that personality is constructed. The other element of the interpersonal aspect of personality focuses on our capacity to observe ourselves. In part, we construct our own personalities.

When a personality judgement is made it refers to the end product of the construction process. What are the implications of regarding personality as a construction for the techniques of judging people?

Personality judgements, however they are derived, are usually presented in the form of a description composed mainly of trait language. It is important to remember that personality traits do not refer to properties inherent within the individual. The interpersonal, socially constructed nature of traits should not be ignored. This suggests that personality judgements should not be based exclusively on information obtained about any one of the elements of personality in isolation. The personality assessor must abandon the search for the one technique that will hold the key to an accurate and objective assessment of personality. Instead, an understanding of personality will be achieved by obtaining a wide range of information about a person from a wide variety of sources. In particular, the value of the person's self-assessment should not be discounted. It is not necessary to construct elaborate questionnaires in which people are asked to report on themselves without guessing what precisely is being measured. When people are asked to give accounts of themselves, the end-product is a useful addition to other information about them and should not be dismissed as suspect. By viewing personality as a social construction, many problems in personality assessment evaporate; but, as with any reconceptualization, a new set of problems will doubtless emerge.

References

1. Child, I. L., 'Personality in culture', in E. F. Borgatta and W. W. Lambert (eds), *Handbook of Personality Theory and Research*, Rand McNally, Chicago, 1968.
2. Hampson, S. E., *The Construction of Personality: An Introduction to Experimental Personality Research*, Routledge & Kegan Paul, London, 1982.
3. Shaver, K. G., *An Introduction to Attribution Processes*, Winthrop, Cambridge, Mass., 1975.
4. Ross, L., 'The intuitive psychologist and his shortcomings: Distortions in the attribution process', in L. Berkowitz (ed.), *Advances in Experimental Social Psychology*, vol. 10, Academic Press, New York, 1977, pp. 173–220.
5. Bruner, J. S., 'Going beyond the information given', in H. Gruber *et al.* (eds), *Contemporary Approaches to Cognition*, Harvard University Press, Cambridge, Mass., 1957.
6. Berger, P. L. and Luckmann, T., *The Social Construction of Reality*, Penguin, Harmondsworth, 1966.

7. Wells, B. W. P., *Personality and Heredity: An Introduction to Psychogenetics*, Longman, London, 1980.
8. Wilson, E. O., *On Human Nature*, Harvard University Press, Cambridge, Mass., 1978.
9. Maslow, A. H., *Toward a Psychology of Being*, Van Nostrand, London, 1968.
10. Eysenck, H. J., *The Biological Bases of Personality*, Thomas, Springfield, Ill., 1967.
11. Eysenck, S. B. G. and Eysenck, H. J., 'Salivary response to lemon juice as a measure of introversion', *Perceptual Motor Skills*, vol. 24, pp. 1047–53, 1967.
12. Harré, R., *Social Being*, Rowman & Littlefield, Totowa, NJ, 1979.
13. Schneider, D. J., 'Implicity personality theory: A review', *Psychological Bulletin*, vol. 79, pp. 294–309, 1973.
14. Bromley, D. B., *Personality Description in Ordinary Language*, Wiley, Chichester, 1977.
15. Shweder, R. A., 'Likeness and likelihood in everyday thought: Magical thinking in judgements about personality', *Current Anthropology*, vol. 18, pp. 637–58, 1977.
16. Nisbett, R. E. and Ross, L., *Human Inference: Strategies and Shortcomings of Social Judgement*, Prentice-Hall, Englewood Cliffs, NJ, 1980.
17. Eysenck, H. J., *The Structure of Personality*, Methuen, London, 1953.
18. Cattell, R. B., *The Scientific Analysis of Personality*, Penguin, Harmondsworth, 1965.
19. Nisbett, R. E. and Wilson, T. D., 'Telling more than we can know: Verbal reports on mental processes', *Psychological Review*, vol. 84, pp. 231–59, 1977.
20. Storms, M. D. and Nisbett, R. E., 'Insomnia and the attribution process', *Journal of Personality and Social Psychology*, vol. 2, pp. 319–28, 1970.
21. Shrauger, J. S. and Schoeneman, T. J., 'Symbolic interactionist view of self-concept: Through the looking glass darkly', *Psychological Bulletin*, vol. 86, pp. 549–73, 1979.
22. Bem, D. J. and Allen, A., 'On predicting some of the people some of the time: The search for cross-situational consistencies in behaviour', *Psychological Review*, vol. 81, pp. 506–20, 1974.
23. Turner, R. G. and Gilliland, L., 'The comparative relevance and predictive validity of subject generated trait descriptions', *Journal of Personality*, vol. 47, pp. 230–44, 1979.
24. Kenrick, D. T. and Stringfield, D. O., 'Personality traits and the eye of the beholder: Crossing some traditional philosophical boundaries in search for consistency in all of the people', *Psychological Review*, vol. 87, pp. 88–104, 1980.
25. Goffman, E., *The Presentation of Self in Everyday Life*, New York, Doubleday Anchor, 1959.
26. Jones, E. E., Davis, K. E. and Gergen, K. J., 'Role playing variations and their informational value for person perception', *Journal of Abnormal and Social Psychology*, vol. 63, pp. 302–10, 1961.

3. Conventional techniques: An industrial psychologist's approach to the assessment of managers

D. MACKENZIE DAVEY

This chapter is concerned with the more conventional methods of judging people in a systematic way. It discusses some of the techniques used by many psychologists and goes on to describe the approach and procedure adopted by the author to assess individual candidates for senior positions in industrial and other organizations. Finally, a managing director who has had the experience of going through such a procedure describes his reactions to it, and another chief executive explains why his company uses the services of a psychologist when appointing, or promoting, senior managers.

The underlying assumptions

The psychologist bases his approach to judging people on three main assumptions:

- That certain personal characteristics are stable, and subject to measurement
- That these can best be 'measured' by a *combination* of techniques
- That the training and experience of the psychologist makes him best equipped to use these techniques

The techniques include different kinds of interviews and a range of 'tests'. (This term covers questionnaires, etc., to which there are no right and wrong answers, as well as intelligence and aptitude tests.)

Characteristics measured and instruments used

Intelligence

One of the classical, and useful, models of the structure of human abilities poses that there is a general factor that is present in everyone to a greater or lesser degree. Those who have it to a very high degree are described as geniuses or intellectually brilliant; at the lower end of the scale are those who might be called dull or moronic. This factor is the ability to learn, the ability to discern relationships, the ability to solve problems, and it is commonly called intelligence or general ability. (The term 'IQ' has, through popular usage, become more or less synonymous.) It is something that can be measured by the most highly developed of all the psychologist's tools.

The history of intelligence testing goes back much further than many people appreciate. It could be said to have started soon after the middle of the nineteenth century with the work of Galton, whose interest in heredity—and especially in the inheritance of intellectual ability—led him to devise methods of measuring individual differences and to provide quantified data; Galton established the first psychometric laboratory in the 1880s.

The historical background is complex, but the important result is that today psychologists have at their disposal tests of intelligence that are both reliable and valid. Accepting that intelligence exists and can be measured, is it of importance to success in management? Given the definition outlined above—the ability to discern relationships and solve problems, etc.—the common-sense answer to the question must be 'yes'. Common sense is not an infallible guide, but in this case it is supported by the findings of various research studies. For example, Bray and Grant[1] identified a 'general effectiveness' factor, which correlated with management career progress; this factor includes 'above-average intellectual competence'. Muller,[2] in a search for qualities essential to advancement in a large industrial group, identified a so-called 'helicopter quality'. Associated with this characteristic are:

- The ability to look at problems from a higher vantage point
- The urge to place facts and problems within a broad context
- The ability to do this by immediately detecting relevant relationships within systems of wider scope

Further support for the general proposition came from a review by Campbell et al.[3] of a large number of actuarial and clinical studies of managerial effectiveness, and from a special study conducted by Ghiselli.[4] In a survey of the validity of various occupational aptitude tests, Ghiselli[5] found that correlations between intelligence test scores and management performance measures increased with the seniority of the positions involved.

Intelligence, as defined by psychologists, is not necessarily accompanied by originality or by 'common sense'; and very often intelligence tests results need to be used not in isolation but in the context of information about attainments, personality, motivation, etc. However, the fact that intelligence tests do not measure or, indeed, give any information about these other characteristics is no reason for rejecting them. They are still useful measures of potential; as Eysenck has said:

> We make use of a hammer in spite of the fact that we cannot use it as a saw or for measuring the strength of an electrical current; it is difficult to see why we should reject intelligence tests because they measure intelligence rather than various other qualities which may also be important.[6]

How well does the average interviewer assess a candidate's intelligence? It is common experience that he or she does it badly, but with great confidence: a dangerous combination. While it is a relatively easy matter to conclude that a man or woman with a first class degree in mathematics and a Fellowship of the Royal Society is 'bright', what of the person with limited education: how able is he? Many of the apparent signs are misleading: the lively, outgoing conversationalist is generally rated higher than the shy introvert; the highly educated person is rated as necessarily cleverer than the one who may not have had the same educational opportunities; a successful business record is taken at its face value; even the person who wears glasses may be judged to be more intelligent than the one who does not.[7] (On this last point, the experimental evidence indicates that with many judges the effect is a short-lived one; the author has encountered a rather alarming number of senior industrialists who stress the importance they attach to their first impressions of people.)

The psychologist aims to discover not only how intelligent a person is but how effectively he or she applies his or her basic ability in various contexts. Many relevant tests are available. Some involve the manipulation of numbers, some call for reasoning in a purely verbal framework. Some mean working under pressure of time; in others the individual can work at his own pace. Some consist of concrete, clearly defined problems and provide all the facts that are needed for their solution. More subtle tests ask the subject to consider non-factual issues: to weigh abstract arguments, for example, or to identify logical errors in propositions put to him. (The man who deals incisively and accurately with concrete problems sometimes falls back on his intuition, on his personal feelings, or on preconceived views when confronted with problems that are less black and white. There is evidence that successful executives are able to be more logical and objective than are the less successful ones.[8])

The psychologist has access to a lot of data on such objectively scored tests; and he or she can, for instance, compare an individual manager's performance with those of large numbers of other managers of similar age, education, etc. Other tests in the intellectual area may not lend themselves to mechanical scoring: for example, those calling for the exercise of imagination or creativity. With some of these the psychologist needs previously to have examined closely the responses of a great many people to the same tests if he or she is to make comparative judgements of such qualities as originality and fluency of thinking.

Personality

The judge, layman or psychologist, usually aims to assess the complex matter of personality by considering more or less clearly defined separate aspects, or factors, and then coming to an integrated view of the individual.

Personality factors that commonly appear on selectors' lists of characteristics to be assessed include:

– Emotional toughness and resilience
– Self-confidence and decisiveness
– Readiness to work hard/activity level

- Flexibility: capacity to adapt to changes, to turn readily from one matter to another
- Assertiveness/dominance and independence
- Friendliness/sociability
- Sensitivity to others' feelings
- Objectivity

Again, research findings[3] support the view that such factors are relevant to management success.

In assessing these aspects the layman has to rely on the information he gets from an interview or a series of interviews and from 'references' given by, e.g., previous employers, and on his observations of the person's behaviour.* Careful interviewing, in particular, can provide valuable data—and there is evidence that trained interviewers make more accurate judgements of people than untrained interviewers.[9] Even so, the majority of psychologists use other tools in addition such as personality questionnaires.

Indeed, some psychologists, concerned to be as objective as possible, rely almost exclusively on such instruments in making their assessments of personal traits. But most would probably agree with Cattell and Kline:[10]

> we should not advocate in either selection or guidance the mechanical use of these procedures [personality questionnaires such as Cattell's 16 PF]. This is because the reliability and validity of the tests, although good, is not perfect, so that in the individual case there is room for error. . . . we would always want to ensure that the results were appropriate by careful interviewing.

Cattell and Kline go on to say: 'This is not to elevate the interview above tests but simply to recognize that it can provide a useful amplification for test scores.'

Most conventional personality questionnaires either invite the respondent to agree or disagree with a series of statements about the way he behaves/feels/believes or ask him more direct questions about such things. There is now considerable evidence that in some situations (such as that of being an applicant for a job) people may be motivated—consciously or unconsciously—to present themselves in what they see as a favourable light.[11,12,13] Many psychologists therefore tend to be wary of placing undue weight on the results of such questionnaires in the selection context. But even when they present a picture that is consistent with all other evidence, the psychologist still has, at times, a difficult task in interpreting them. There can

---

* The 'stress interview' is sometimes employed, more by lay interviewers than by psychologists, in an attempt to judge how a person will behave under pressure. The candidate is often treated with deliberate rudeness, or even aggression, and his response to this is noted by the interviewer. The author believes that this is neither a socially acceptable technique nor necessarily a valid one: the way an individual may behave when subjected to artificial stress can be very different from his reaction to real-life pressures. (There would appear to be almost no published work providing evidence for the validity of the stress interview.)

be almost countless permutations of factors. To take some greatly over-simplified combinations:

Intelligent	Stable	Introvert
Intelligent	Unstable	Introvert
Intelligent	Unstable	Extravert
Less intelligent	Unstable	Extravert

and so on . . . all very different types of people. And the psychologist may be having to consider permutations of as many as 20 factors (and varying levels of each factor).

Interpretation of such data calls for a sound understanding of personality theory and much experience. And even greater experience and psychological insight is needed for a second group of personality tests, the projectives. In these the individual may be shown a series of pictures (or the well-known Rorschach inkblots) and asked to produce stories about them; perhaps more commonly, he may be presented with the beginnings of a series of sentences and asked to complete them. The hypothesis is that the person's responses reflect aspects of his personality; someone who ends a sentence beginning 'Often I . . .' with 'feel frightened and inadequate' contrasts strongly with the one who puts 'think there are no limits to what I can achieve'. These are extreme examples; but a sensitive psychologist can often learn a great deal from less obvious responses.

A management assessment programme

The following procedure, which is that followed by the writer, is fairly typical of the way industrial psychologists go about assessing managers, or potential managers.

The individual, who may be a short-listed external candidate for a senior position, an internal candidate for a specific promotion, or a young manager being considered for an expensive training course, is invited by the company concerned to spend the best part of a day with an outside professional adviser. To reduce the air of mystery/magic, he is usually given in advance some details of what will happen. (Some companies have printed leaflets outlining the procedure and explaining why they use it, what they expect to get out of it, and what the individual concerned can expect to get out of it in the way of subsequent 'feedback'.) The first item on the programme is always a preliminary informal talk with the psychologist. This has two functions: first, to make sure that the person knows what the day's programme is going to consist of and that he or she understands the objectives of the whole exercise; second, to reduce any tension. The psychologist's aim is to get across to the person that he is not going to be subjected to such experiences as 'stress interviews' and that there is no question of his passing or failing on the various paper-and-pencil tests he will be doing. The person then spends some hours working on the tests; he or she also has an interview with the psychologist.

This interview, which is central to the programme, is conducted as an informal, unstructured discussion; there are no questions probing into private matters. The person is asked in essence to describe his life history: a task which, after possibly a little initial embarrassment, most people enjoy.

If there is a technique involved in this kind of interviewing it is a technique of listening, of stopping oneself from interrupting, of tolerating pauses while the person thinks about how to describe what happened next, of asking open-ended questions[14] and subtly encouraging him or her to talk freely. In this kind of interview, attitudes and opinions will inevitably emerge as well as facts; and the interviewer is listening for the former as well as for evidence of recurring themes or patterns or behaviour in the life history. (The man who has consistently made major decisions for himself in the past is likely to continue to do so in the future; the man who has always led an essentially solitary life is unlikely to change into a highly gregarious person, even if his personality test results suggest that that is how he would like to see himself.)

At the end of the day, all the data are assembled: test scores, profiles from personality questionnaires, responses to projective tests, interview findings, and anything else judged relevant. (The last may include observations of unusually nervous or apologetic or aggressive behaviour during the day.) In making his judgements, the aim of the psychologist is to construct a 'model' (inevitably an over-simplified one) of the person that can be used to predict how he will behave at work. The report eventually produced will not go into the *causes* of any behaviour thus predicted; it may say 'He will be a cautious decision-maker', but it will not say 'because he had acute fears of falling at an early age he has been left with a strong need to avoid risk and so will be a cautious decision-maker'; it may say 'He is drivingly ambitious', but it will not go on to say 'in compensation for feelings of inferiority resulting from a deprived background'. The report to the company describes the person's style in three main areas of functioning.

1. *Intellectual effectiveness.* Basic intellectual capacity (compared with other managers). Quick learner? Conceptual thinker? Numeracy? Verbal skills: ability to communicate in speech? in writing? An objective thinker? or much influenced by his emotions? Able to produce original ideas? Imaginative? Strictly conventional?

2. *Work style.* Generalist or detail-minded? Sense of priorities? Decision-making approach: impulsive? cautious? slow? confident? Strategist—long-term planner? Tactician? Flexible? Energetic? Highly restrained? Not vigorous but efficient? Tolerance for pressure: stable? high risk? Reaction to emergencies: calm? flustered? Ambitions: how important to him? will he sacrifice other interests? are his aims realistic? Flexibility: can he handle a number of tasks in parallel? Adaptability: can he adjust to different environments?

3. *Personal relationships.* Relationship with boss: frank? amenable? stubborn? loyal? Relationships with peers: friendly? co-operative? tolerant? a team person? highly competitive? a loner? Relationships with subordinates:

domineering? protective? decisive? sensitive? willing to delegate? Relationships with outsiders: confident? careful? disdainful? courteous?

A summary at the end of the report includes a list of what appear to be the person's major assets and main limitations in relation to the needs of a particular job. A recommendation may be made about the suitability of his *personal* characteristics for a specific position (it is obviously not the psychologist's job to assess his technical qualifications or his work experience). Alternatively, a general assessment of his potential may be given.

The report also usually contains a short section pointing to any major development needs and suggesting specific ways of meeting these, such as particular training courses or reading programmes. It may also include advice for the individual's boss on the style of management he is likely to respond to. (Does he need a good deal of support and encouragement? or close control? or to be given a degree of independence?)

Feedback

Some psychologists consider that an offer of feedback, a discussion of the main findings with the person, is almost an ethical requirement: the individual is *entitled* to this discussion with the psychologist. In a typical feedback session the latter will not only advise the person on how to capitalize on his strengths but will also give him some counselling on how he might develop, or compensate for, or come to terms with, his 'weaknesses'. Candidates almost invariably welcome this open 'warts and all' discussion, and the knowledge that they are entitled to it gives the whole assessment procedure a positive appeal. Managers already established in their organizations often *ask* to have a psychological assessment so that they will have more evidence to help them think about, and plan, their careers.

In conclusion: The other side of the coin

Perhaps the most common reaction of a manager* to the prospect of going through an assessment programme is one of apprehension: he possibly feels that he has been 'hoodwinking' the world about his competence for a long time and that he may be going to be caught out at last! Another reaction comes from the manager who knows that she is likely to be appointed to a more senior job and is concerned about whether she is really up to it (although she may not admit this to her employers); such a person will often genuinely welcome the view of an independent outsider. Then there is the man who initially announces a little belligerently that he has 'been with the company for ten years and they ought to know all about me', or the one who declares that his qualifications, or his record, should be good enough evidence for any new

---

* The reaction of a senior manager to the experience of going through the assessment programme outlined above is described on p. 34.

employer. (These people usually admit, after their preliminary apprehension has subsided, that a good record at one level, or in a particular company or industry, does not necessarily mean that they will be successful in more senior positions or different environments.) The fear of failure, while it is often unwarranted, is perhaps more common than is generally realized; and assessment findings often provide valuable reassurance to those who go through the procedure.

A managing director's reactions to assessment: The seventh veil

Michael Bardsley, Managing Director, Dun & Bradstreet Ltd

'Oh . . . I should have mentioned it before, but would you mind spending a day with our headshrinker?' The managing director shifts, deliberately relaxed, in his chair, puts his head back and looks out of the window. 'Of course, it's a formality, you know—all our candidates go through it; in fact, all my senior managers have been through it. I am sure you will find it a most interesting experience.' The eyes are slightly steely as they return to meet your gaze.

Reactions are varied. I have been in both seats. My personal reactions as interviewee included: *resignation*: the inevitability of finding skeletons you had carefully packed away; *interest*: finally to see ourselves as others see us; *stimulation*: as you lift the hammer to ring the bell at the fun fair; *concern*: how competent will the blighter be?

Sitting behind the desk, I have observed: *indignation*—'Doesn't my record speak for itself?'; an unsaid expression indicating 'Are you not sufficiently confident of your own interviewing technique?'; genuine momentary *fear or anger*. But in my experience such reactions are rare. The bulk of people who reach the short short-list for a senior management position have sufficient objectivity and confidence in themselves to recognize that independent professional analysis is a necessary adjunct to the selection process; and that at worst the feedback will be useful to them in self-development and career planning.

There is such a thing as 'form'. In examinations, on social occasions, in selling situations, in the management of people and things, there are days when you are at your best or your worst—and you know it. I know too that the professional analyst largely disputes this. But I would still maintain that irrelevant skeletons can loom larger than life and the intellect can slip out of gear on bad days. When the sun is shining, the perspective is balanced and the mind incisive.

My own particular day was a fine one. Prompt at 9.00 a.m. I rang the doorbell of a London house and was ushered into the lion's den. This is probably the key: he was no lion. More than 20 people who have shared and compared this experience with me agree that, within minutes, defensiveness has evaporated as you are led delicately through your life, apparently inconsequentially. Occasionally you realize the significance attached to a chance remark three sentences back, like eating a chilli when you thought it was a French bean. The psychologist takes notes with the earnestness of a secretary fresh from school. The facts of your life? Not a bit of it: his perceptions of your perceptions.

An hour and a half flies by in easy conversation. Then, casually, he glances at his watch and says 'Now, how about a few of my little tests?' And the day moves into higher gear. Gentle reminiscence is replaced by challenge.

Timed tests probe your numerical, verbal, spatial, and imaginative capabilities. You search the recesses of your mind for long lost algebra. You wish you had pitted your wits against verbal wordpower in *Reader's Digest* more frequently.

For a time your intellect is left to relax and you are then moved down to the seat of your emotions. In a space of 20 minutes you place your tick against 200 sets of alternatives. (Would I really prefer to be a grave-digger than a fan dancer?) With a drink in your hand several hours later, with most of the alternatives still clear in your mind, you realize the interconnections of the alternatives placed before you and understand the significance of the whole, despite the absurdity of the part.

A second cut at the emotions: in your own time, you are asked to complete a series of wide-open sentences. Irrelevantly, you wonder how many marks you lose for bad grammar. You ponder on the significance that can be attributed to the innocent choices you finally make.

Then back to the intellect: but this time the shift is from intelligence to judgement, the point where intellect and emotion meet. You are presented with four case histories and asked to pronounce judgement on a series of questions relating to them. As in life, not all the facts are present. Deduction is necessary before judgement can be made.

The day is now almost at an end. Ten minutes with your benign persecutor, in which he mentally tests your pulse rate and calculates your loss of weight, and you totter out into the sunlight.

Reflecting on the day, you realize the thoroughness of the check-up. You see the relevance of the tests. Intelligence testing—verbal, numerical, spatial—is public property in paperbacks, publicly discarded as being a poor yardstick for ability. And so it is, as a single yardstick. Many people excel at all three types of test and yet achieve little success. However, the successful who do not excel at at least one of them are very few. You realize that the connections between your reminiscences when sitting on a comfortable sofa and the attitudes you displayed when choosing which alternatives to tick must have more than a little solidity. The marriage of intellect and attitude in the judgement you displayed after analysing the case histories must complete the jigsaw puzzle. The only remaining question in your mind is the competence of the assessor himself.

Two days later you have a chance to find out. The assessor is assessed. You return for your 'feedback'. You may be, as I was, genuinely nervous. Is the market really the best place in which to stand naked? The shaving mirror is bad enough. Self-knowledge is a fine thing, in theory, but look what it did for Adam!

Back again to that comfortable sofa. The psychologist reads you his judgement on this case history: you. You learn how your basic intelligence compares with that of the management population. You learn about your powers of critical thinking; the breadth of your imagination; your strengths and weaknesses in dealing with people: your peers, your seniors, and your subordinates; how you react in team situations, under stress; your work capacity. Around this skeleton of fact and judgement he has sculptured the softer tissues of attitude and personality. You trace back many of his comments to your discussion. You are surprised that he has picked on some points and left others, which you believed significant, untouched. You are surprised that the picture he has built up resembles very closely your own appreciation of yourself. The gentle guidance he gives you to self-development you knew already but, probably, had rarely given sufficient attention.

As you leave, you are confident that your assessor has removed six of the veils; but there is always the nagging doubt that the seventh is removed only for your would-be employer.

Why my company uses psychological assessments

Mark J. Souhami, Chairman, Dixons Photographic (UK) Ltd

In common with most companies, we had always made management appointments on the basis of interviewing people. Usually the programme would consist of an initial interview, which resulted in a second short-list interview, and sometimes a final third interview, before appointment. Almost invariably, when making appointments either from within or outside the Company, there was a tendency to hire people who were moving upward and were thus being, to a greater or lesser extent, promoted.

As with most employers, our record of success was patchy, not only because of our variable success in selecting people, but also because of the way in which the successful candidates were managed during the first months of their appointments. The act of filling the vacancy tended to have a cathartic effect, and the manager appointed was often given a period of time to settle in. Thus it was only comparatively recently that we came to realize that it is the way in which the manager is himself managed in the first weeks and months of his appointment that has a large influence on his success. This, coupled with the fact of the costs of recruitment and the salaries paid for senior management are extremely high, led us some three years ago to seek outside guidance as to how we should improve our selection procedures. After all, we would not undertake major building works without professional advice, nor would we install plant and machinery without engineering advice. However, here we were quite cheerfully employing people and using selection methods based entirely on our own experience and without any independent evaluation.

After considering many possible alternatives, we were attracted by the industrial psychology approach. In order to form our own judgement of its effectiveness, we sent for trial assessment a selected band of employees whom we knew, mainly long-service and senior, whose strengths and weaknesses we thought were apparent. The resultant reports surprised us by their accuracy. The results achieved from an in-depth interview plus testing gave a profile of the individual which in many cases had taken us years to build up ourselves. As a result of this 'test marketing' we determined to pursue this route in making senior appointments in future. However, before doing so all directors were asked to submit themselves to the screening process so that they themselves might have an understanding of what was involved and also would appreciate how they might use the reports, both in making selection decisions and in the early days of managing the newly appointed candidate.

Since then the results have been most useful. A number of candidates who came close to being appointed were not, but these were the minority. In most cases the screening has confirmed our opinion and has given the candidate, through feedback, a better and more independent insight into the company he would be joining and the management environment in which he would be operating. Senior managers have settled down more quickly as a result, and their superiors have been able speedily to get the most out of the new investment.

SPECIMEN REPORT

Mr A. B. Smith

Confidential Assessment

by

D. Mackenzie Davey

This is a *Confidential* management report.

It should be shown only to those responsible for making decisions about the individual concerned. Under no circumstances should it be shown to him or its contents discussed with him.

PERSONAL MAKE UP

Note: This report is concerned primarily with judgements about how the candidate will behave at work. It does not concern itself with the reasons why he will behave in any particular way; nor does it comment on technical or professional competence.

INTELLECTUAL EFFECTIVENESS

Note: Comparisons are made below with the 'management population'. This is a highly selected group of senior managers who represent, in terms of their intellectual capacity, approximately the top seven per cent of the general population.

Synopsis

Mr Smith's basic intelligence places him a little below the average for managers.

(i)   *Numerical*
      He worked quickly but inaccurately on a numerically based reasoning test and
      his score was below average—at a level which would be bettered by two out of
      three managers.

(ii) *Verbal*
      His score on a test of verbal comprehension was substantially above average.
      He has a large vocabulary which he deploys effectively in both speech and
      writing. His fluency is impressive and could lead to an over-estimation of his
      intellectual power.

(iii) *Logical*
      On tests of various aspects of 'critical' thinking his performance was
      undistinguished and placed him well below the management average. He is a
      man who tends to allow his feelings to influence his judgement: he would
      have more difficulty than most managers in analysing them objectively and
      dispassionately. He will act on intuition and frequently allow his personal
      views to influence his judgement.

(iv) *Imaginative*
      He responded fluently to tests of 'productive' thinking and produced an above-
      average number of ideas. The evidence suggests that, faced with novel or
      unexpected problems, he will not be at a loss and he could produce some
      imaginative ideas.

WORK APPROACH
(i)   *General approach*
      He is an energetic man who tackles his work with vigour and drive.

(ii) *Mastery of detail*
      He does not see it as important to have a thorough knowledge of the minor
      matters for which he is responsible. Indeed, in order to achieve what he saw as
      his primary objectives, he would tend to dismiss many matters as trivial or as
      irrelevant detail.

(iii) *Productivity*
      He is hard-working. He is able to sustain his efforts and will generally put
      through a good deal of work in a comparatively short time: his output will be
      high.

(iv) *Quality of work*
      He can work faster than most managers, and he will sometimes sacrifice
      accuracy for speed; thus, although his output will be substantial it will not
      always be of the highest quality.

(v)   *Decision-making*
      He is optimistic and rather impetuous. He will make swift positive decisions.
      Those concerned with concrete, tangible problems will usually be sensible, but
      his judgement on matters of policy or broad strategy must be suspect.

(vi) *Tolerance for pressure*
      Mr Smith does not appear to be well equipped to work under extended
      pressure. He is not emotionally robust and his capacity to tolerate more than
      moderate stress is questionable. He will act swiftly, but not always
      intelligently, in a crisis.

(vii) *Flexibility*
There is a restlessness in his make-up which gives him the flexibility to adapt to new situations and to accept changes of priority without complaining. But the same restlessness makes him bored with routine work and intolerant of tasks calling for steady application. This factor has probably contributed to his relatively frequent job changes over the last twelve years.

(viii) *Ambition*
He is ambitious and prepared to make sacrifices in order to progress. He hopes to be chief executive of a medium-sized organization or to have a senior executive role in a large one—both are a little unrealistic. He can, in the right environment, be a competent middle manager, but he is unlikely to be successful in a top position.

RELATIONSHIPS WITH OTHERS

(i) *General impact*
Mr Smith uses his verbal skills to present himself positively, but he tends to be a little over-zealous in displaying his charm and, especially over longer periods, is likely to be seen as rather superficial in his personal relationships. Thus, while first impressions can be excellent they may not be sustained.

(ii) *Relationships with superiors*
His seniors will find him a mixture of amenability and stubbornness. He will communicate his views lucidly and often contribute constructively, but there will be times when he will be unable to conceal his anxiety and will behave in an ill-judged manner. He could, for example, appear frivolous at inappropriate times—he uses laughter to escape from difficult situations—and at other times he will be obstinate and aggressive.

(iii) *Relationships with peers*
He would not be a particularly good man in a team; he is inclined to be over-critical of the views of his associates and over-sure of the rightness of his own judgement. Moreover, he would become impatient if subjected to the delays imposed by committee work. He is action-centred and he becomes frustrated and irritable if unable to implement his ideas.

He lacks the stability and personal security to develop mature relationships. Most especially, his high degrees of sensitivity will lead him to see slights where none are intended and to treat the most neutral of situations with suspicion.

(iv) *Relationships with subordinates*
He would make earnest efforts to manage others with authority but may not always be able to sustain his status. He has underlying doubts about his own capacities and these will sometimes become evident in his direct dealings with subordinates. On the other hand, he would often be seen as a positive and cheerful manager, and, when not obsessed with his own feelings and sensitivities, would show an awareness of the problems of others. Moreover, his instructions will be lucid and unambiguous.

PRIMARY ASSETS

Industrious and energetic
Flexible; can adapt to change
Decisive
Above-average ability to communicate clearly
Imaginative
Makes a good first impression

PRIMARY LIMITATIONS

Basic intellectual power a little below average
Judgement of emotionally toned situations suspect—analytical skills below average
Unstable and insecure—doubtful capacity to tolerate extended stress
Hypersensitive—quick to take offence
Unable to sustain seemingly friendly, cheerful manner
Not at his best in a team

GUIDELINES FOR DEVELOPMENT

Mr Smith needs the support of a well structured environment and clearly defined duties to give him stability. His methods of working and limits of authority should be agreed in advance. He should be encouraged to develop his analytical skills: he will never be a gifted logician but he could become rather less subjective in his judgements than he is at present.

SUMMARY

Mr Smith has many admirable characteristics—in particular, his energy and drive, his communication skills, and his decisiveness. Against these must be weighed his distinctly limited emotional stability and his modest intellectual resources.

He presents himself skilfully but he is unable to sustain the positive impression that he makes. In his efforts to do so his manner comes to appear rather forced and false. Moreover, he is an extremely sensitive man who would detect in the most innocent of actions or statements by others a criticism or even an insult. In consequence, his relationships with his associates are likely to deteriorate considerably.

Handling familiar tasks, he could be relied upon to act sensibly and incisively. This often impressive performance could lead to a general over-estimation of his abilities and the temptation to give him more demanding duties which would, in many cases, be beyond him. He is very close to his limits, and while he could do a competent job at one stage higher than his present one he is unlikely to be effective in top positions.

References

1. Bray, D. W. and Grant, D. L., 'The assessment center in the measurement of potential for business management', *Psychological Monographs*, vol. 80, 1968.
2. Muller, H., 'The search for the qualities essential to advancement in a large industrial group: An exploratory study', (anon. company), The Hague, 1970.
3. Campbell, J. P., Dunnette, M. D., Lawler, E. E. and Weick, K. E., *Managerial Behaviour, Performance and Effectiveness*, McGraw-Hill, New York, 1970.
4. Ghiselli, E. E., *Explorations in Managerial Talent*, Goodyear, California, 1971.
5. Ghiselli, E. E., *The Validity of Occupational Aptitude Tests*, Wiley, New York, 1966.
6. Eysenck, H. J., *Uses and Abuses of Psychology*, Penguin, Harmondsworth, 1953.
7. Argyle, M. and McHenry, R. 'Do spectacles really increase judgements of intelligence?' *British Journal of Social and Clinical Psychology*, vol. 10, pp. 27–9, 1970.

8. Starch, D., 'An analysis of the careers of 150 executives', *Psychological Bulletin*, vol. 39, pp. 7, 1942.
9. Anstey, E., *An Introduction to Selection Interviewing*, HMSO, London, 1977.
10. Cattell, R. B. and Kline, P., *The Scientific Analysis of Personality and Motivation*, Academic Press, London, 1977.
11. Vernon, P. E., *Personality Assessment*, Methuen, London, 1964.
12. Albright, L. E., Glennon, J. R. and Smith, W. J., *The Use of Psychological Tests in Industry*, Scandinavian University Books, Copenhagen, 1963.
13. Cronback, L. J., *Essentials of Psychological Testing*, Harper & Row, New York, 1959.
14. Mackenzie Davey, D., and McDonnell, P., *How to Interview*, British Institute of Management, London, 1975.

4. Assessment centres

CLIVE FLETCHER

In terms of thoroughness, time, cost, and, some would say, effectiveness, the assessment centre is the Rolls-Royce of psychological assessment. The term 'assessment centre' (AC) covers a wide range of procedures used for a variety of purposes, but basically it means the assessment of a group of individuals by a team of judges using a comprehensive and integrated series of techniques, such as psychological tests, interviews, simulation exercises, and peer ratings. The purpose of the AC may be recruitment, the identification of management potential, and/or the training and career development of those assessed.

The employment of such an ambitious approach is by no means new. In fact, both the British and German armies[1,2] developed multiple assessment procedures in the 1930s and 1940s for officer selection, and the American Office of Strategic Services used something similar in helping with the difficult task of selecting secret agents.[3,4] Rather less exotically, but with commendable foresight, the method was taken up after the war by the British Civil Service as a means of picking people for (ultimately) senior positions in the Administration group. In one form or another, the Civil Service Selection Board (CSSB) has used it ever since.

What led to ACs being used widely in industry and for purposes other than just initial selection was a study done in the American Telephone and Telegraph (AT & T) Company in the mid-1950s. The 'management progress study',[5] as it was called, set out to follow the careers of a group of young managers and to investigate the changes they went through and the factors that contributed to their success or failure. Bray and his colleagues needed to establish what the abilities and characteristics of their sample were at the outset in order to gauge subsequent changes, so they set up what was in effect an assessment centre. Before long its potential for uses other than research were appreciated, and AT & T began employing ACs in the identification of potential. This sparked off similar schemes in other American organizations, and today they are in widespread use there. Not untypically, Britain, having played a part in pioneering this kind of approach, seems to have been rather slow in adopting it: Gill[6] found that only 4 per cent of 236 UK companies surveyed used ACs for assessing management potential.

The methods used in ACs

As has already been indicated, the purposes of ACs vary, though all have some judgemental function. The constituent elements of an AC will to some extent differ according to what the organization wants to use it for and in line with the nature of the organization's work (e.g., an exercise involving a business plan presentation might have little use for some public sector bodies whose main function is administration). A brief description of the chief methods used in ACs is given below; not all will be found in any one AC, and the list is by no means exhaustive.

Leaderless group discussion

In its simplest, least-structured form, this means sitting the candidates down together, giving them a topic to discuss, and leaving them to get on with it while the assessors sit outside the group and make notes on the ensuing interaction. More often, though, a greater degree of task structure is provided. For example, the candidates may be told that they are a group of senior managers who have to examine the case for re-locating a factory in another part of the country and to advise the board of directors on the advisability of such a move (relevant papers giving background details would be provided for the exercise). A time limit would be imposed on the discussion (usually 30–40 minutes). Specific roles can be allocated to candidates if this is felt to be desirable; for instance, each might take it in turn to act as chairman of a committee (consisting of the other candidates) dealing with a set problem, assuming that ability at this kind of task was relevant to what the candidates were being assessed for. A further important variation is to introduce an element of competition into the situation. Each candidate might be given particular options to advocate: it could be an individual for promotion, a site for a new office, a new line of development for the company etc., and the group would be required to come to an agreed choice of just one of the options. This kind of conflict, between group membership and responsibility on the one hand and the need forcefully to press one's own case on the other, can be very revealing. Each assessor will 'mark' one or two candidates, assessing them on such dimensions as assertiveness, influence, oral expression, and interpersonal skills. Derivatives of Bales's group interaction analysis[7] are sometimes used in the assessors' monitoring of the group's behaviour. For a fuller consideration of the leaderless group discussion, the reader is referred to B. M. Bass.[8]

The in-tray exercise

Typically, this presents the candidate with a mixed series of problems that a manager might find in his in-tray (on a bad day, it might be added!). Some need little more than a signature, but others demand difficult judgements as to whether they should be delegated and, if so, to which of the subordinates described in the supporting brief to the exercise; or whether immediate action is necessary; or simply of what to do to solve the problem. The candidate has a fixed, and probably slightly inadequate, time in which to work through the items, so he is under considerable pressure. How he deals with it all will throw light on his penetration and judgement, analytical ability, handling of subordinates, tact, and written expression (initially, at least, the candidate's response to the problems is written), among other things. A de-briefing session with one of the assessors afterwards is vital, so that the logic, or lack of it, behind the candidate's approach to dealing with each problem can be properly understood.

A parallel of the in-tray (which in American literature is called the 'in-basket exercise') for more administrative-type work might be the use of an extended written problem, such as the British Civil Service Selection Board uses. The candidate is faced with a collection of documents, for example, newspaper reports, transcripts of radio broadcasts, departmental memos, letters from members of Parliament, and others, all relating to some controversial decision that has to be made. The task is to analyse this welter of information, summarize the pros and cons of the various courses of action available, and then plump for one of them, presenting a well argued rationale for the choice made. Again, the time pressure is severe, and the individual's ability to sift the relevant from the irrelevant is thoroughly tested.

For a review of the research on the in-tray, and a useful bibliography relating to it, see R. W. T. Gill.[9]

Role-playing interactions between two people

Some ACs include role-playing of appraisal, counselling, or guidance interviews; this is particularly popular where the candidates are being assessed for jobs in the personnel field, but is clearly appropriate to line management skills as well.

Interviews

The aim of interviews in ACs to some extent depends on who is carrying them out. If it is a psychologist, it will very likely be an attempt at personality assessment, perhaps with particular emphasis on judging the individual's emotional stability, insight and self-awareness, and relations with others. Interviews done by line managers acting as assessors might seek more general information about the individual's career history, his reactions to work of different types, his aspirations and ambitions. Sometimes both types of interview are conducted. The empirical studies of interviewing have shown that this technique has rather poor results[10] when used on its own. This has led some practitioners to drop them from AC programmes. Having experienced ACs both with and without the use of interviews, I have no doubt as to which is the better approach. ACs without interviews can leave you with large question marks about a candidate that have been raised, but not answered, by the other exercises; an interview provides the kind of richness of information that can fill in these gaps in the emerging picture of the candidate. While some of the research findings on the effectiveness of selection interviews suggest that it *might* be unwise to let judgements made in interviews feed into the assessment of a candidate directly—though there is some evidence of interviews making just such a direct contribution successfully[11]—it will impoverish the overall understanding of the candidate gained if the insights potentially offered by interviews are ignored altogether.

Business games

These can be viewed as a special form of leaderless group discussion, though they depart some way from that technique. The candidates are formed into teams, each one representing either a firm or some particular section of the firm. They are then usually required to operate within a given market environment in such a way as to achieve maximum efficiency according to some criterion (often net profit). The team may operate in co-operation or, especially where they 'represent' different companies, competitively. The organizer of the game generally needs access to a computer, since the decisions taken by each group of candidates have to be fed into the computer model and the results of those decisions on production, sales figures, and so on are given back to the syndicates as quickly as possible. The simulation may last some hours, with candidate teams continually analysing the data produced by the computer, taking decisions, looking at the outcome, and revising their strategy. The way the teams are organized varies, but it is probably better not to allocate roles, though the syndicates may do so themselves as part of their coping response if they wish. The time pressure involved in business games can be quite considerable and more than adequate to simulate real-life circumstances. Assessors observe each team in operation and scrutinize the decisions made and their outcomes. The exercise can throw light on leadership ability, numeracy, business sense, and the capacity to organize and get on with other people. If it is used with feedback from senior managers afterwards, it can also clearly be a stimulating learning experience for the participants.[12]

Psychological tests

Tests of ability and of personality are used in many ACs. The ability tests generally cover verbal and numerical facility, though exactly how and in what depth differs widely. Personality tests and questionnaires are less frequently encountered in ACs, but some do use the 16PF (a widely employed questionnaire devised by R. B. Cattell, which measures a range of personality variables) or even projective techniques: tests that present the individual with a vague or meaningless stimulus, e.g., an ink blot, which he has to interpret, the idea being that he 'projects' important aspects of his personality into these interpretations (for a description of such tests, and the problems associated with them, see P. E. Vernon).[13] How such data as are provided by psychological tests should be used in ACs is open to debate, particularly the personality measures. In some it is an integral part of the assessment information; in others it provides only background information. A further possibility is the use of tests as a screening device; putting people through ACs is not cheap, as we shall see, so any way of identifying individuals who, through personality factors (e.g., very high anxiety level) or lack of basic intellectual equipment, are unlikely to profit from the experience can save them some discomfort and the organization some money.

Other exercises and measures

Biographical questionnaires have been found to be useful in American ACs. Properly constructed and analysed, they have shown quite good predictive ability in terms of who is and is not likely to be successful in management (again, like psychological tests, such questionnaires may be used as a screening device for pre-selection). Self-description is another popular self-report device; the candidate might be invited to describe himself first through the eyes of a friend and then through the eyes of a critic. Information of this kind is sometimes useful when followed up in an interview, but should always be treated with caution; it reflects how the individual sees aspects of himself (or how he wants the *assessor* to see him), not necessarily how anyone else will see him. This latter perspective can be provided in part by peer ratings. It is common practice for candidates on an AC to be asked to rate or rank each other in terms of whom they would most like as a boss, as a colleague, and (sometimes) as a holiday companion. This gives some insights into the dynamics of the candidates as a group that assessors are not always aware of, and is a useful piece of information on each individual's interpersonal relations. However, mixed-sex groups can be a difficulty here, as female candidates will usually be rated as first choices of holiday companions (if only because the male candidates are worried about the inferences that might be made about them if they do not choose a woman). Moving to more objective procedures, individual exercises feature in many ACs. A drafting test, in which the individual might be asked to write a difficult letter calling for firmness and tact, is an example, as would be a business presentation, in which the candidate makes an oral presentation on some topic (e.g., the company's sales strategy in the next few years) to one or two of the assessors. Exercises of this kind test communication skills of different kinds. Finally, there are special techniques developed by individual companies to assess qualities they think are particularly vital. For instance, a test of 'perceptive listening' is used by at least one organization. Here the candidates watch a detailed, not particularly interesting film and are then tested on the amount of information they have retained. This could arguably be as much a test of memory capacity and motivation as of ability to listen.

The major techniques used in ACs have been described. The number used in any centre ranges from 4 to 40, with a mode of 7.[14] For examples of how they are combined together in a programme, and indeed of how they are operated overall, the reader is referred to Gill, Ungerson, and Thakur,[15] Williams,[16] Stewart and Stewart,[17] Moses and Byham,[18] and Dulewicz.[19]

Running an assessment centre

Having looked at the constituent elements of an AC, it is appropriate to consider the equally basic questions of who is assessed, by whom, on what dimensions, where it takes place, and what the information gained is used for.

The candidates

They number anything from 4 to over 80, but most often are in the range of 5–12. Who the candidates are naturally differs according to whether the AC is used for initial selection or for the identification and development of management potential. In the latter, the problem is deciding the best method of saying who should or should not attend the AC. The candidate pool is usually made up of the lower management levels (though occasionally it takes in some more senior staff, too) and specialist or technical staff who may wish to move into general management, or whom the company wishes to assess for management potential within their specialism. They may in some cases be self-nominated or nominated by their managers. Not all organizations allow self-nomination, though disallowing it would seem to reduce true equality of opportunity. Nomination by supervisors or managers has the disadvantage of sometimes making nominees feel that they are obliged to attend the centre, while not all of them may wish to do so. Supervisory nominations will be based on the individual's record to date and so could also be made centrally by any organization operating a worthwhile appraisal system.

The assessors

These are almost invariably senior managers, often assisted by one or more occupational psychologists and, sometimes, external consultants. The number will vary according to the number of candidates at each AC; the normal assessor–assessee ratio is in the region of 1:2 or 1:3. The managers should be of sufficient seniority to have substantial experience of the levels they are assessing potential to reach and, with any other assessors employed, should be able to perform this task regularly over some reasonable period. A commitment of this kind is necessary if standards of assessment are to be consistent from centre to centre. It is also important in maintaining the quality of the individual assessor's performance. Unfortunately, because of the demands made upon any senior manager's time, this level of commitment is not always easy to get, and it is perhaps a fair barometer of both the assessor's and the organization's belief in the value of ACs, and indeed in management development generally. Maintaining assessor performance is one thing, but getting that performance to an acceptable level in the first place is quite another. In those instances when assessors are given little or no training, the quality of the judgements made will probably be extremely variable. I fondly remember the (admittedly extreme) example of an untrained assessor observing a leaderless group discussion exercise (part of an AC run by a major brewery group for graduate recruitment) and offering a string of highly favourable ratings on a female candidate who had said no more than two sentences in the half-hour discussion; when challenged, he said he felt that she *knew* what to say but simply did not actually say it! Training should aim at eliminating 'mind-reading' of this kind, though genuinely clairvoyant assessors would be most welcome. The training might include doing some of the exercises as an assessee, assessing videotaped exercises, and discussing the ratings made with colleagues and trainers (usually consultants and psychologists) afterwards, and sitting-in as an observer on actual ACs. The first run as a 'live' assessor should follow on the training as soon as possible.

The assessment dimensions

How the assessment dimensions are arrived at varies, but it is often (too often) a subjective process, senior managers stipulating what abilities and qualities they feel are essential to effective functioning at higher levels. Ideally, some attempt at a comprehensive job classification of senior posts[20] and an analysis of those jobs would be made. The classification element is desirable, as it may well be that different groups of jobs will require rather different managerial abilities, which can be taken into account in the assessment. Thus, an individual might be found to be rather low on some abilities but have compensating qualities that fit him well for advancement in a specific direction. Other, less ambitious, methods of arriving at the most appropriate set of dimensions exist; for a discussion of these see A. Stewart and V. Stewart.[17]

This chapter has in a sense put the cart before the horse; for convenience of presentation the content of ACs has been described before the nature of the assessment dimensions. In actually setting up an AC, it is essential to ascertain what the relevant dimensions are at the outset, because they determine which exercises are appropriate to include in the procedure (for instance, it would be pointless having a drafting exercise if 'expression on paper' was not judged to be an important dimension of ability for higher management jobs). The candidates are not assessed on every dimension on every exercise, but the assumptions as to which exercises give evidence of which abilities or qualities are largely based on subjective, intuitive judgements.

The number of dimensions of assessment, like most other aspects of ACs, vary enormously. In the original management progress study, a set of 25 qualities was drawn up.[21] Most present centres probably use fewer, and it could be argued that man's limited information-processing capacity makes it difficult for anyone effectively to use as many as 25 dimensions independently. Sophisticated statistical analysis of the ratings made at four ACs have shown that raters are really using a much more limited set of dimensions, summarized by M. D. Dunnette[22] as:

– Overall ability and general effectiveness
– Organizing and planning (administering)
– Interpersonal competence (human relations ability and understanding)

– Cognitive competence (intellectual and quality of thinking)
– Work orientation (motivation)
– Personal control (control of feelings, resistance to stress)

Research in other areas of psychology also suggests a limitation on the number of dimensions that can be used effectively.[23] So a typical list of the attributes assessed at an AC might look something like this one from Standard Telephones and Cables AC:[19]

– Analytical ability
– Helicopter ability
– Administrative ability
← Business sense
– Written communication
– Oral communication
– Perceptive listening
– Vigour
– Emotional adjustment
– Social skill
– Ascendancy
– Flexibility
– Relations with subordinates

Where ACs are run

Usually ACs are run in hotels with suitable facilities (large rooms for group sessions, plenty of small syndicate rooms, photocopying and office support services, etc.). They can be run in-company, though many would argue that it is beneficial to remove everyone from the 'normal' work environment: it perhaps reduces the chances of people trying to contact assessors about matters that have come up in the office, and provides a setting that is equally new to all candidates (negating any benefit that some might get from the AC being held, for instance, at headquarters if they normally worked there while other candidates did not).

What the information is used for

Generally, ACs last anything from three days to a week. The last day is devoted to the assessors' conference, at least in part. The object is to pull together all the information obtained on the candidates, iron out any minor inconsistencies or differences in opinion between raters, and come to a final assessment. The latter may simply be in terms of accept/reject in selection, or it may be an overall rating of management potential. Each candidate and his performance is reviewed and discussed thoroughly; if there is fundamental disagreement between assessors, this should be allowed to stand rather than attempting to coerce one or more of them into agreement. The conference will normally be presided over by a member of top management, and it may sometimes be left to him to give the 'casting vote' in particularly difficult cases. A vast amount of information is gathered on each candidate over the course of the whole AC process; while we are concerned with it here mainly in the context of assessing or judging people, to use such information solely in this fashion is wasteful. Many organizations use the data to assist in the individual's career development, irrespective of whether he has been adjudged to have high potential; indeed, some use it only for counselling and development functions rather than for any kind of selective assessment. This, therefore, becomes an element in the assessors' conference, and any company career development specialists should be present. At some point, preferably soon after the AC, the assessments made should be fed back to the candidate, either by one of the assessors or by a psychologist. This can be difficult, especially if the candidate did not do very well in the exercises and tests, and requires high-level counselling skills. The aim is not simply to get the candidate to accept an assessment—no easy task, as any appraisal interviewer will tell you [24,25] but also to give his reactions and feelings about the AC, which may throw some light on his performance, and to enlist him in planning the development activities appropriate to the profile of abilities that has been revealed. Whether the candidate's line management is involved in this process, and whether any of them see their actual assessment report from the AC, varies according to the organization; certainly some degree of participation by the individual's manager in evolving and implementing the development plan is at least desirable and probably necessary.

The reliability and validity of assessment centres

This approach to assessment clearly demands a substantial investment of time and money. Does it produce commensurate results? Looking at reliability first, or the consistency of the judgements made, between different assessors the level of agreement or similarity of ratings achieved has generally been very satisfactory.[26] Inter-rater reliabilities—correlations between raters' scores for candidates—vary from exercise to exercise but average around 0.75, which is very high. In a study at IBM, Greenwood and McNamara[27] found that psychologists and managers showed roughly the same level of agreement with each other in assessing candidates. While the type of assessor might make little difference, the quality being assessed does, and there is some evidence in the literature of differing reliabilities for different dimensions; H. A. Thomson[28] found that the reliability for ratings of 'drive' was 0.74, while for the 'amount of participation' it was as high as 0.93, reflecting almost perfect agreement among the judges. So reliability in this sense is certainly adequate; but in terms of the procedure as a whole producing the same set of scores and ratings for a candidate going through it on two separate occasions there is little evidence. Perhaps by the nature of the exercise people seldom attend the same AC twice, so it is difficult to get data on those that do. Resorting here to personal experience, I have been struck by the similarity of the assessments made by completely different judges, using the same procedures, on those (admittedly few) candidates seen attending a recruitment AC for the second time. On the other hand, there are salutary examples of candidates whom I have seen do very well on their second AC appearance, having done rather poorly on a previous time ranging from one to five years before. This does not imply that the raters were wrong in their initial assessment; the evidence suggests that the candidates improved their performance second time round. How or why they did this is something that needs researching: clearly, some candidates do not make the best of the first opportunity. It has been argued[29] that some candidates do not acquit themselves well in selection interviews because of inappropriate attitudes, inadequate experience, or misleading expectations: perhaps something similar happens in more extensive assessment procedures, too. Whatever the explanation, it seems imperative that candidates are not 'written off' following an unsuccessful showing at an AC. Indeed, it might be best if any individual had the right to nominate himself more than once, though maybe not more than two or three times.

Reliability is important, but does not of itself guarantee a great deal. It might be said, for example, that at one stage in history the judgement that the world is flat had a high degree of reliability; the fact that people agree on something does not of itself guarantee that they are right. Validity, the extent to which an assessment procedure actually does measure what it purports to, is the more important attribute. Assessment centres do look as though they are measuring what they set out to measure; as Gill *et al.*[15] say, this face validity of the procedure is almost frighteningly high. We need much more substantial proof than simple appearances provide. A number of studies have shown that AC ratings correlate well with other criteria of effectiveness, e.g., supervisor's ratings, salary progress, promotions.[30] There is evidence that AC performance predicts career success over a long period.[31] But valuable as this evidence is, it does not conclusively show the AC's predictive powers; in some cases, the follow-up data are available only on those who get through an AC procedure used in selection, while in others the results of the AC were known to line managers, which raises the possibility of a 'self-fulfilling prophecy' effect being operated. Perhaps the best and 'purest' study was the original one done by Bray and Grant[21] at AT & T. The assessment data were *not* made available to managers or supervisors, or even to the 110 participants: they were not acted on at all, until between five and eight years later when the predictions made at the AC were compared with the actual career progress made by the individuals concerned. It was found that, of those predicted to reach middle management, 42 per cent did so and only 4 per cent had remained at the same grade as the time they attended the AC. Of those who were predicted to make no progress above the entry grade, 42 per cent were in accordance with the prediction and only 7 per cent did better than expected by reaching middle management.[22]

The largely favourable research findings on ACs do not automatically confer validity on any such centre that is set up. All of those researched to date have had much care and considerable resources put into them, including the use of trained assessors. Organizations setting up ACs and wishing to emulate the record of the best-known examples (including those of AT & T and the

Civil Service Selection Board) would have to demonstrate similar commitment. Ideally, that includes evaluation research, establishing inter-rater reliability, and validity of both the constituent elements of the assessment centre and of the overall ratings that come out of it.

Now, if this kind of long-term investment in assessment centre methodology is contemplated, the question may be not just of overall validity of the approach, but of its cost-effectiveness. The actual cost per candidate obviously varies with the length of the AC, the assessor–candidate ratio, the use of hotel or in-company assessment, and so on. For an idea of the sums involved, see Stewart and Stewart[17] and Gill et al.[15] While the costs and the potential benefits can be quantified with varying degrees of precision, what is difficult to estimate is the extent to which ACs are cost-effective in comparison with other simpler methods. The suggestion has been made, by Ungerson[30] among others, that, where the candidates are drawn from the existing workforce of the company, there may be more effective ways of using the existing information about them which would produce comparable results at less expense. The idea is that a proper appraisal scheme, which is still one of the main ways of assessing potential that is used,[32,33] along with psychometric tests might provide an accurate predictor of future performance and capacity. MacKinnon[26] cites evidence that tends to show ACs as being superior to more conventional methods, but for reasons of methodological weakness these studies are not conclusive. However, the problems of devising really effective appraisal schemes[34] are such that this approach might end up being just as costly as an assessment centre—though it would of course serve a day-to-day management function as well as judging long-term potential.

A perspective on assessment centres

This chapter has sought to give the flavour of the assessment centre method, if anything that varies so much can be defined as a single method. It has necessarily been brief, and anyone wishing to read about the topic in greater depth should look up the references given already, along with Finkle.[35] On the evidence so far, this approach has immense promise. It certainly presents problems, as has been hinted at already. Not least of these are the dangers of prematurely dismissing an individual's level of potential, or of creating 'crown princes' (the individual is identified as having potential and thus gets such special treatment and promotion that the whole thing becomes a self-fulfilling prophecy). More research is needed on such things as the extent to which previous job experience influences AC performance, whether the candidate's expectations and attitudes make any difference in how well he or she copes with it, and how successful women are compared to men in ACs (though here it is worth pointing out that the American Equal Opportunities Commission approves of the AC method). Yet enough is known to justify greater use of the approach than is presently made of it in the UK. Is the lack of enthusiasm due to the costs incurred, or does it go deeper and reflect a lack of commitment to management development as a whole?

Finally, the use of assessment centres initially concentrated on meeting the organization's needs to make judgements about people. Even then, the reactions of the assessees seems to have been largely favourable.[36] Attempts have increasingly been made to capitalize on the method's potential as a learning and development experience from which the participants can actively benefit, both in terms of contributing to their own assessment and making use of the information subsequently in their personal career planning. Perhaps this is the most creative contribution made by this method, and other approaches to assessment may find it a helpful example.

References

1. Morris, B. S., 'Officer selection in the British Army, 1942–45', *Occupational Psychology*, vol. 23, pp. 219–34, 1949.
2. Simoneit, M., *Grundriss der Charakterologischen Diagnostik*, Teubner, Leipzig, 1944.
3. Murray, H. A. and MacKinnon, D. W., 'Assessment of OSS personnel', *Journal of Consulting Psychology*, vol. 10, pp. 76–80, 1946.
4. OSS Assessment Staff, *The Assessment of Men*, Rinehart, New York, 1948.
5. Bray, D. W., Campbell, R. J. and Grant, D. L., *Formative Years in Business: A Long-term AT and T Study of Managerial Lives*, John Wiley–Interscience, New York, 1974.
6. Gill, D., *Appraising Performance: Present Trends and the Next Decade*, IPM Information Report no. 25, Institute of Personnel Management, London, 1977.
7. Bales, R. F., *Interaction Process Analysis: A Method for the Study of Small Groups*, Reading, Mass., Addison-Wesley, 1950.
8. Bass, B. M., 'The leaderless group discussion', *Psychological Bulletin*, vol. 51, pp. 465–92, 1954.
9. Gill, R. W. T., 'The in-tray (in-basket) exercise as a measure of management potential', *Journal of Occupational Psychology*, vol. 52, pp. 185–98, 1979.
10. Schmitt, N., 'Social and situational determinants of interview decisions: implications for the employment interview', *Personnel Psychology*, vol. 29, pp. 79–101, 1976.
11. Grant, D. L. and Bray, D. W., 'Contributions of the interview to assessment of management potential', *Journal of Applied Psychology*, vol. 53, pp. 24–34, 1969.
12. Elgood, C., *Handbook of Management Games*, Gower Press, London, 1976.
13. Vernon, P. E., *Personality Assessment: A Critical Survey*, Methuen, London, 1963.
14. Bender, J. M., 'What is "typical" of assessment centres?' *Personnel*, vol. 50, pp. 50–7, 1973.
15. Gill, D., Ungerson, B. and Thakur, M., *Performance Appraisal in Perspective*, IPM Information Report no. 14, Institute of Personnel Management, London, 1973.
16. Williams, R., *Career Management and Career Planning*, HMSO, London, 1981.
17. Stewart, A. and Stewart, V., *Tomorrow's Managers Today*, Institute of Personnel Management, 2nd edn, London, 1981.
18. Moses, J. L. and Byham, W. C., *Applying the Assessment Center Method*, Pergamon Press, New York, 1977.
19. Dulewicz, S. V., *IMPACT: The STC Assessment Centre*, Standard Telephones and Cables Ltd, London, 1979.
20. Dulewicz, S. V. and Keenay, G. A., 'A practically oriented and objective method for classifying and assigning senior jobs', *Journal of Occupational Psychology*, vol. 52, pp. 155–66, 1979.

21. Bray, D. W. and Grant, D. L., 'The assessment centre in the measurement of potential for business management', *Psychological Monographs*, vol. 80, entire issue, 1966.

22. Dunnette, M. D., 'Multiple assessment procedures in identifying and developing managerial talent', in P. McReynolds (ed.), *Advances in Psychological Assessment*, vol. 2, Science and Behaviour Books, Palo Alto, California, 1971.

23. Bannister, D. and Mair, J. M. M., *The Evaluation of Personal Constructs*, Academic Press, New York, 1968.

24. Fletcher, C., 'Interview style and the effectiveness of appraisal', *Occupational Psychology*, vol. 47, pp. 225–30, 1973.

25. Fletcher, C. and Williams, R., 'The influence of performance feedback in appraisal interviews', *Journal of Occupational Psychology*, vol. 39, pp. 75–83, 1976.

26. MacKinnon, D. W., *An Overview of Assessment Centres*, Technical Report no. 1, Center for Creative Leadership, Greensboro, North Carolina, 1975.

27. Greenwood, J. M. and McNamara, W. J., 'Inter-rater reliability in situational tests', *Journal of Applied Psychology*, vol. 31, pp. 101–6, 1967.

28. Thomson, H. A., 'A comparison of predictor and criterion judgments of managerial performance using the multitrait-multimethod approach', *Journal of Applied Psychology*, vol. 54, pp. 496–502, 1970.

29. Fletcher, C., *Facing The Interview*, Unwin Paperbacks, London, 1981.

30. Ungerson, B., 'Assessment centres: a review of research findings', *Personnel Review*, vol. 3, pp. 4–13, 1974.

31. Anstey, E. 'A 30-year follow-up of the CSSB procedure, with lessons for the future', *Journal of Occupational Psychology*, vol. 50, pp. 149–59, 1977.

32. Holdsworth, R. F., *Identifying Managerial Potential*, BIM Management Survey Report 27, British Institute of Management, London, 1975.

33. Anstey, E., Fletcher, C. and Walker, J., *Staff Appraisal and Development*, George Allen & Unwin, London, 1976.

34. Fletcher, C., 'Performance appraisal', in D. Guest and T. Kenny (eds), *Personnel Techniques and Personnel Strategy*, Institute of Personnel Management, London, 1982.

35. Finkle, R. B., 'Managerial Assessment Centres', in M. D. Dunnette (ed.), *Handbook of Industrial and Organisational Psychology*, Rand McNally, Chicago, 1976.

36. Kraut, A. I., 'Management assessment in international organizations', *Industrial Relations*, vol. 12, pp. 172–82, 1973.

5. Interviewing

ROWAN BAYNE

Nearly all selection and assessment procedures include some kind of interview, a fact that seems generally to be accepted, tolerated, or taken for granted. Other responses include an outright rejection of the interview as a worthwhile technique;[1] the perhaps more considered belief that interviews by trained and cautious interviewers have a moderate level of validity some of the time, and that some further improvements may be possible;[2,3] and the more speculative view that interviews might be dramatically improved, that little is known of the limits of interviewing.[4]

These very different responses to interviewing as a way of judging people are based on the personal experience of the author and on interpretations of research. The general finding from research following up the predictions of interviewers is that they usually fail. However, several factors come between the prediction (this person will do the job well, or best) and the successful candidate's actual job performance. For example, a clear and precise job description may well not have been available. If it was not, then failure to predict performance at work cannot justly be attributed to the interview. At the very least, the interviewer was handicapped. Moreover, even if a good job description was available, performance at work is influenced by other people, the economic climate, life outside work, and so on.

A related difficulty in interpreting the interview's 'failure' is the controversial state of personality theory: presumably, not having an adequate idea of what one is trying to judge in an interview is a handicap to judging it well. Two other aspects of the research, though, are more positive. First, some interviewers have, or appear to have, succeeded in judging people.[5,6] Second, interviews and interviewers vary greatly, for example, in terms of length, structure, qualities assessed (interviews), and in terms of personality, other personal qualities, and amount, quality, and recency of training (interviewers). This means that some kinds of interview, interviewer, or both may be relatively useful for assessing some personal qualities; for example, stable, middle-aged women (other, more exotic, qualities are of course possible) may be particularly good at judging stability in young men applying for a certain kind of job.

More general uses of selection interviews may also be valid, but at the moment whether these exist or not is unknown. (The few positive studies may be flawed, or freaks). On the other hand, the case for trying to discover the limits of interviewing seems to be quite a strong one. The point about variety has already been made: an interview is not a standard technique, like a questionnaire, and the fact that interviewers affect interviewees' behaviour, which seems obvious, has not been sufficiently recognized in selecting, training, and studying interviewers.

The flexible nature of interviews is both a danger and a strength. On the one hand, it can be abused, when a candidate is asked leading questions, for example; and on the other, it can mean a greater chance of counteracting a central problem in personality assessment: faking. Indeed, the skilled interviewer's ability to detect and overcome faking is itself justification for continuing to try and improve interviewing.

This is not to say that psychology will never devise personality tests that are more effective than most or all interviewers, or that all present tests are useless for selection (i.e., compared with research or counselling). Rather, it is to say that interviewing is potentially strong in an important respect, while all methods of judging people so far devised, and as far as is known, have weaknesses. For example, application forms assume we are 'prisoners of our past'; and 'unobtrusive measures'—like measuring with a special chair how restless a person is, or determining which magazine in a waiting room a candidate reads, or even which pages—are hard to interpret; the candidate may have read the magazine of most interest already. Such procedures are not ethically straightforward, either.

I should like to emphasize that selection interviewing as currently practised presents a gloomy picture, as is indicated in some of the studies discussed later in this chapter, and by Schmitt's[6] list of suggestions for the 'practising personnel interviewer'. These include deciding what the purpose of the interview is to be and allowing the candidate time to talk! If interviewers in general need such reminders, then spinning a coin is better, both on grounds of efficiency and by law. The legal aspect is likely to be increasingly important, and interviews should not be seen as a way of avoiding validation of selection techniques: the detailed implications of the Sex Discrimination Act (1975) and the Race Relations Act (1976) are being worked out in court, but tests are illegal if they discriminate unfairly. Moreover, in American law interviews are tests,[7] and of course a biased interview is by definition unfair (as well as inefficient), hence the point about spinning a coin.

So far I have argued that interviewing is potentially a powerful way of judging people, and in particular is the method most likely to counter people's ability to fake. Like all the techniques available, it has worked sometimes (i.e., successfully predicted behaviour) but has faults: interviewing is especially likely to be taken for granted and abused. Above all, the limits of interviewing are not known. Two analogies may be helpful here. First, Webster[8] remarked that if people can learn such an unusual skill as proofreading, then there is hope for interviewing too. He was arguing that, just as proofreaders overcome the apparently automatic process of reading for meanings, so interviewers can resist those aspects of 'normal' person perception that interfere with good interviewing, e.g., being most attracted to people who are like ourselves, judging people on their age or race, assuming that people are more similar to ourselves than they really are. Second, Randell[9] suggested that, as currently practised, interviewing may be like golf played with a 24-handicap. For those unfamiliar with golfing terms, this is an optimistic view, allowing considerable scope for improvement.

Both analogies focus on the interviewer, as does nearly all the research. Interviewees and kinds of interview are other possible sources of information bearing on the limits of interviewing. In this chapter I shall discuss recent approaches to these three aspects of interviewing: respectively, interviewer training and the concept of effective listening; candidates' reports on inter-viewers, and candidates' beliefs and strategies; and an experiment comparing board and sequential interviewing.

These approaches range from the immediately practical to the very speculative, the latter in harmony with this book's emphasis on the less conventional. I shall discuss the approaches mainly with reference to selection interviewing, but with other forms of interview (there being considerable overlap) in mind. The final section touches on a model of selection interview-ing perhaps best called a counselling skills approach, with the emphasis on skills. The term implies that the literature developed for the many kinds of professional interviewer—psychiatrists, police, social workers, bank managers, etc.—should be integrated. However, discussion of a few approaches is preferred here to what would be a catalogue.

Interviewer training

In a recent review of training in general, Hinrichs[10] remarked scathingly that the emphasis is usually on generating programmes rather than on defining problems, on appearance rather than on trying to make a real difference: 'the good programme is attention-getting, dramatic, contemporary, or fun. Whether or not it changes behaviour becomes secondary'. Part of the problem is that there is little concern with using theory, let alone with building new theory. Moreover, there is very little research on the effectiveness of training: its survival and growth are based on faith. Yet Hinrichs considers that trainers do some things well and that improvement is possible (a) by understanding those good things and then applying the principles more widely; (b) by developing a better psychology of training—at present we have only tired and not very helpful recommendations like 'Motivate the learner' and 'Distribute practice'; and (c) by evaluation using more than simple questionnaires ('happiness sheets'), and perhaps even using control groups.

Several current approaches to training interviewers are concerned with defining problems and with making a difference. Lewis, Edgerton, and Parkinson,[11] for example, try to develop a relatively undefensive group as a preliminary to learning interviewing skills, and include training in some basic counselling skills—a point to which I shall return. Second, Davison[12] described a highly structured course covering the skills of (a) gathering information, (b) assessing the information, and (c) decision-making. Each of these skills is divided into separate behaviours and learned first 'as an isolated unit'. Davison also emphasized the importance of separating decision-making from assessment, and of justifying assessments by citing 'specific, objective evidence'—which, however questionable the term 'objective', has the merit of not placing the tutor in the role of omniscient judge as well as being important in its own right.

Third, Maguire and Rutter[13] were concerned with improving communication between doctors and patients, and in particular with the initial history, i.e., with doctors gathering accurate and relevant information from a patient new to them. They began by studying videotapes of such interviews between senior medical students and co-operative, articulate patients, and found numerous deficiencies, including failure to pick up cues, repetition, asking leading questions, and, perhaps ironically, acceptance of jargon, e.g., taking at face value a statement like 'I feel depressed'. The results were very clear; e.g., 74 per cent of the students were rated as poor or very poor at picking up verbal leads, while 24 per cent failed to discover the patient's main problems.

Maguire and Rutter also tested the medical students' interviewing skills in a real outpatient clinic, and found the same deficiencies. Their next step was to devise a training programme and to test its effectiveness. Their course was a 45–60-minute individual tutorial for each student in which one of the student's interviews was replayed and discussed, and compared with a handout on interview structure, the information that should be obtained, and the techniques that should be used. Their evaluation of the training used as a criterion the amount of relevant and accurate information obtained by trained and untrained students respectively. These results too were very clear: the trained students obtained nearly three times as many relevant items.

In a further study Maguire and Rutter considered whether one component of the training programme was the most powerful: perhaps simply reading and discussing the handout was as effective, for example, as this plus the videotape. So they compared the programme with videotape feedback and the programme without. Only a small difference (in favour of the video group) was found, too small to be of practical significance; the implication is that something other than video made the difference; against the experimenters' expectations, but in line with the views of Lewis et al.,[11] who regard video as too cumbersome for short courses. On the other hand, only one aspect of interview performance was assessed, and video feedback may have an important part to play in teaching ways of developing 'rapport', relevant to doctors as an influence on, for example, whether patients follow advice or not, and to selection interviewers for the public relations aspect of their role. Maguire and Rutter envisage further developments of their research programme, concerned, for example, with group training and with *when* interviewing skills are learned most successfully. It seems to me a model approach.

The interviewer's state of consciousness

Maguire and Rutter's research was concerned with several interviewing skills. I should like to turn now to what may be an underlying factor in good interviewing, a 'master variable': the interviewer's state of consciousness and its possible relationship with effective listening. I think this notion is worth developing and testing, though it is far more speculative and less immediately practical than the approaches to training discussed so far.

By effective listening I mean encouraging candidates or interviewees to talk as well as they can, and truthfully, and perceiving their personalities accurately. These two aspects of good interviewing are interdependent: candidates who feel encouraged will probably provide better information than those who do not, while interviewers need to see candidates accurately in order to encourage them successfully. The idea is to try and establish what Argyle[14] calls 'an atmosphere of timeless calm', to put both interviewer and candidate in the right frame of mind for the interview.

For the interviewer, this means avoiding distractions—it helps, as in other activities, to be unselfconscious when interviewing, at least most of the time— and the ideal state of mind for this seems in theory to combine calmness and alertness. To expand on this possibility: the calm–alert state is seen as promoting rapport, with the interviewer's calmness helping the candidates to relax and his or her clear perception allowing productive silences and the easy asking of questions. The state also counteracts habituation to interviews, when the interviewer is calm but bored. And it allows intuitive processes as well as the usual thinking, evaluating, ones.

I think good interviewing—effective listening—requires this unusual state of consciousness; it involves several activities and the capacity to carry them out either simultaneously or by switching easily from one to another. At times the good interviewer is sharp and in focus, specific and rational; at other times intuitive, picking up nuances and rationalizations; at others stepping back to see the whole interaction, fitting things together and also taking note of the amount of time left and the areas to cover. The good interviewer is, or would be, doing more than this, but the description indicates something of the complexity, strain, and exhilaration of good interviewing.

Meditation seems to be one way of achieving or enhancing a calm–alert state. Several people have reported responses to meditation exercises of extreme calmness, alertness and lucidity, though they may, of course, be deceiving themselves. Wright,[15] for example, described a week in a meditation centre. He was in very quiet surroundings with a meditation master and a small group of other students. Between 5.30 a.m. and 11 p.m. they did ordinary things, like eating and walking about the centre, very slowly. For between six and ten hours a day they 'just' sat very still. This would have been very boring for an observer, but Wright found that inside himself there was a 'silent uproar'. His task was to observe this uproar and allow it to happen. He too suggested several stages of meditation, but the important point here is the apparent effects of this procedure. After two days there was 'a state of considerable relaxation and clarity', and Wright felt a greatly enhanced sensitivity, including really seeing and listening to others. Moreover, these apparent effects seemed to last for about six weeks of 'normal' life (as a professor of education) before gradually fading.

Meditation, however, has at least one drawback: it appears to require steady and prolonged practice. A set of mental exercises developed by Harding[16] provides an alternative approach, and the practical results of research with the approach are easy to imagine: an interviewer taking a few minutes to do an exercise, becoming calm and alert for the 30 minutes or so of the interview (the ratio of 6:1 is based loosely on Wright's experience), and thereby listening more effectively to someone who might also have done a mental exercise.

I am investigating one of those exercises at the moment.[17] It may seem bizarre, or even nonsense. Mental exercises in the Zen tradition *are* nonsense, deliberately so. Consider, for example, the well-known exercise of trying to imagine the sound of 'one hand clapping'. It does not have a rational solution, which is the point; it is intended to reduce the dominance of an analytic, verbal mode of consciousness, and to give an intuitive, holistic mode of consciousness more scope. The idea is that both ways to knowledge are useful and complementary. Harding's exercise has a similar aim, at least in part, but is also based directly on a theory. So I will outline part of the theory and then the exercise.

Harding sees what he calls the 'face game' as very widespread in our society, using 'game' in Berne's *Games People Play* sense, as a way of being in the world that interferes with open communications and accurate perceptions. At one level the notion of face game describes doing things in order to impress others: the reverse of 'being natural' or at ease. The possible application of improvement to interviewing is obvious.

At another level Harding takes the term 'face' more literally. He argues that part of the face game is to pretend you have a face when, in a certain state of consciousness, you do not experience yourself as having a head, let alone a face. He calls this the 'first person' state, when a person is truly inside looking out. And he believes that people are born first person and gradually are 'turned around' so that they become third person, and in a sense outside themselves. Harding is not saying that first person is rare and good, third person is common and bad. Rather, he feels that both views of self are valid but that the first person, like the intuitive, holistic mode of consciousness, has been over-shadowed: ideally, people should be 'consciously both first person and third without confusing them'.

His exercises are very simple, perhaps deceptively so, and their aim is to redirect your attention to the first person singular, to become unaware that you have a face and head. Harding asks you to point to your feet, then your legs, and so on. He asks, 'What is your finger pointing at?' When you reach your head he asks, and the wording is very precise, 'On *present* evidence, on your experience *now*, what is your finger pointing at?' And as a supplementary question: 'Is it like peering through two little holes in a kind of meatball? If so, what's it like in there—dark, stuffy, congested, small?'

An important point about Harding's exercise is that the first person state of consciousness, which is associated with calm–alertness, is obvious once experienced, but it is also elusive. As Harding says, it does not really exist as a memory or an idea: it has to be experienced.

I said that the exercise, and its variations, might seem bizarre. In any case, the question of whether they work or not, i.e., produce a calm–alert state, is an empirical one.[17]

The candidates' views

There have been relatively few studies of candidates (or clients, or interviewees). Keenan and Wedderburn,[18] and Fletcher,[19] provide two new perspectives in this approach to improving interviewing. Keenan and Wedderburn, like Maguire and Rutter in the research described earlier, wanted to study how interviewers obtain information, in their case from candidates rather than patients. They noted that there is a lot of written material on what interviewers *should* cover, much of it of dubious value, but that how interviewers *actually* behave is not clear. They considered three methods of collecting data about interviewer behaviour in real-life interviews: using a trained observer, asking interviewers, and asking candidates. The first two methods were rejected, as likely to change the interviewers' behaviour, and they chose to ask candidates immediately after their interviews.

Several interesting findings emerged: for example, that, according to candidates, interviewers often failed to probe initial answers, especially where there was a possible weakness, and that a direct approach was used more than an indirect. A direct approach to the question of how socially skilled someone may be is to ask 'Do you get on well with people?'—in effect, asking the candidate to judge him or herself. An indirect approach means asking about relevant past behaviour, looking for evidence of social skill or lack of it, with the interviewer making the judgement and the chances of successful faking reduced.

Another fault, as reported by the candidates, was that interviewers tended to ask questions about things they—the interviewers—were familiar with: their organization rather than the student's work, or reasons for taking particular subjects. This suggests that the interviewers were more concerned with their own psychological comfort than with judging the candidate accurately. Again, there are clear indications for improving interviewing skills, and for increasing our knowledge of the limits of interviewing as a way of judging people.

Fletcher[19] asked candidates what they believe about selection interviews, and what strategies they adopt, with the idea that, in part, such strategies and beliefs are likely to affect candidates' behaviour in an irrelevant way, and therefore to interfere with accurate judgements by the interviewer. Thus, some candidates may believe that directness and honesty are good strategies, others that there are ways of putting things without actually lying. Fletcher found quite considerable disagreement among candidates on some questions of belief and strategy, and reasonable consensus on others. They disagreed, for example, on the statement, 'Interviewers make up their minds about accepting or rejecting most people in the first five minutes or so' (59 per cent said true, 41 per cent false); they tended to agree that 'they had to be completely honest with the interviewer' (71 per cent). Generally, their views were more varied: thus, 36 per cent agreed, 23 per cent were uncertain, and 41 per cent disagreed with the statement, 'One should try to project a particular "image" of the sort of person you would like the interviewer to think you are.' Overall, there seemed to be a preference for an honest and co-operative approach but with marked individual differences. If the subjects in Fletcher's study behave in accord with their reports, the quality and amount of information gathered by interviewers will be strongly affected. A candidate who smiles a lot, is open about his areas of weakness, and volunteers information will present a very different picture from a candidate who thinks she should be serious, mention weaknesses only if pressed, and not volunteer information.

(*Wrong!*)

A crucial element in Fletcher's argument is that these beliefs and strategies are *not* seen as related to personality characteristics in any systematic or general way. This itself is an empirical question; meanwhile, it seems to me that, with candidates employing different strategies and interviewers playing safe (to simplify), it would be remarkable if accurate judgements were made on much more than a chance basis. Indeed, the picture of selection interviews as charades or rituals is supported. However, it also seems clear that quite simple training methods can make a real difference, as discussed earlier. Fletcher suggests, in addition, training candidates and letting them know in advance the topics to be discussed.

Two types of interview

Type of interview may also matter. With two colleagues,[20] I have carried out an experiment comparing the two most widely used types of selection interview: the board or panel, in which a candidate faces several interviewers at once, and the sequential interview, with the candidate meeting a series of interviewers, one at a time. We asked: 'Other things being equal, does the type of interview in this structural sense make a difference? Or is it a trivial variable, overwhelmed by individual differences in interviewing skill?'

There is general agreement that board interviews are less relaxed than one-to-one interviews and that therefore less useful information is obtained from or provided by candidates. Argyle[14] treats this as self-evident. On the other hand, some interviewers and candidates may find the greater intimacy of one-to-one interviews threatening, which might reduce the amount of useful information gathered. Moreover, a board interviewer will probably ask crisper questions; and, perhaps the most powerful argument in favour of board interviews, the tasks of asking questions and observing are shared, and might therefore be done more efficiently (see Anstey[3] for further discussion).

Our experiment was designed to provide preliminary evidence on the relative efficiency of the two kinds of interview. There are, of course, variations of them, e.g., using interviewers with very different interviewing styles. We looked at semi-structured interviews, with three-person boards, and series of sequential interviewers, and the interviewers were trained and very experienced. We used the following criteria to compare the two kinds of interview:

– More useful information obtained from candidates
– More accurate assessment of a personal quality
– More positive view of the interviewers, and themselves, by candidates
– More positive view of the interviews, and themselves, by interviewers

To take these in turn, Anstey[3] argued that, when writing a report, an interviewer should take pains to distinguish between established facts and inferences from facts. General statements about the candidate's personality traits or attitudes should not be made on flimsy evidence. And they carry more conviction if supported by specific examples of his characteristic behaviour, for example, 'He is an enterprising person who has enjoyed planning holidays abroad for himself and his friends.' On this view, interviewers are seen as more likely to consider and perhaps to improve their assessments if they are asked to give reasons for them.

Some alternative views are (a) that some interviewers' intuitive judgements may be the most accurate; (b) that it is pointless to ask interviewers to say why they made a particular judgement; and (c) that requiring interviewers to cite evidence for their judgements will lead to a new definition of good interviewing: the ability to rationalize. Selection interviews would then be a ritual, and concerned with the appearance of rationality. In any case, in the experiment we asked interviewers to cite evidence, and this, as noted earlier, is likely to become a legal requirement soon. Indeed, an adequate record will probably be needed of areas covered, evidence collected, and interpretations made.

The other criteria of efficiency were more accurate perception of a personality trait, and the attitudes of interviewers and candidates to themselves and to the interviews. Here we were interested in the public relations aspect of interviewing: organizations want good candidates to accept their offer of employment, and all candidates to leave with a positive impression of their selection procedures and, by implication, of the organization. Briefly, we found that type of interview does not make a substantial difference, contradicting some expert opinions.

There are problems with the experiment. One is defining information or evidence. For example, gender is an inference based on evidence like body shape. So if an interviewer rates a candidate as independent-minded and cites as evidence 'sticks to his views, could say why'—is that evidence? Most of the raters thought so, but in my view some examples are needed. A second problem is that the experiment was an exploratory one, and the findings are preliminary and tentative. Apart from anything else, it was the first study in the area, and several compatible results, preferably with variations of interview purpose, candidates, and design, are needed before confidence in the stability of the findings is justified.

A counselling skills approach to selection interviewing

Finally, I should like to touch on a few elements in a counselling skills approach to selection interviewing. This approach assumes that interviewers want to (a) collect relevant information, (b) attract good candidates—who, by definition, and especially at senior executive level, are more likely to have a choice of jobs and organizations; and (c) leave candidates who are not successful feeling they have been treated fairly. Although the interviewer may enjoy 'grilling' candidates and catching them by surprise (torpedoing, as one put it), I think stress interviews are counter-productive in all these respects. Interviewers discover how the candidate behaves in a stress interview, when the stress in the job may well be of a different kind, or trivial; and stress interviews discourage or anger some candidates.

However, the first element in a counselling skills approach comes before the interview and other methods of assessment; this is to inform candidates beforehand about the selection procedure. It is probably both efficient and humane to do this, because candidates' expectations should then be more similar (except for particularly sceptical candidates). Moreover, candidates prefer, and are likely to respond more usefully to, interviewers who are interested in them and who ask technical questions on topics they know about, which includes topics they have been able to prepare for. Again, these are issues on which there is some evidence,[21] and on which more is needed.

Lewis[21] suggested another element in a counselling skills approach, arguing that good selection interviewing shares some of the qualities of good counselling, as far as these are known. If Lewis is right, it follows that selection interviewing would be improved by selecting the interviewers accordingly or through modified training. Lewis did not argue that selection interviewers should see themselves, or behave, as therapists or counsellors; his main concern is with improving validity. Counselling skills currently taught, e.g., active listening, seem to me useful here and likely to lead to candidates feeling appropriately stretched: counselling is not soft and wishy-washy.[22]

Gilmore's approach[23] is the basis of Lewis' argument. She sees good counselling as in part a combination of understanding, acceptance, sincerity, and the ability to communicate these qualities. To understand someone is to grasp fairly clearly and completely what he or she is trying to say: a reasonable aim for any kind of interviewer. Acceptance means allowing others to be different from you by not making value judgements: Gilmore says 'celebrating' the differences. Communicating acceptance in this sense is difficult, but of course interviewers should select the best candidates whether they like them or not. The third quality, sincerity, is particularly hard to define, although in everyday life we judge and refer to it often: 'I really believed him'; 'She puts on such a front'. It is not the same as being unflinchingly honest. I think the main defining characteristics of sincerity in this sense are being aware of one's own experience, as in Harding's notion of the 'face game' discussed earlier, and not making false statements, e.g., 'I see what you mean', when, telepathy aside, it is not possible.

Other elements in a counselling skills approach include the possibility that tests may be taken more honestly; realistic job previews; and telling candidates the reasoning underlying the decisions made about them—at this stage 'counselling' itself is a more appropriate term. Such notions are expensive to put into practice, but then so are having people in the wrong jobs, and bad publicity. They also require highly skilled interviewers, but legal requirements seem likely to enforce this anyway. Assessment centres (see Chapter 4) may be *the* answer, especially if modelled on a counselling skills rather than a stress approach. I think they are efficient in the most pragmatic sense because, by including relatively realistic samples of the job itself, they satisfy present legal requirements. They may also be efficient economically and socially.

Summary and conclusion

Interviewing as currently practised is a poor method of judging people. However, other methods have marked weaknesses too, and there seem to be many possible ways of improving interviewing. Several of these were discussed, in particular some immediately useful approaches to training; the speculative notion of a mental exercise influencing interviewers' states of consciousness; candidates' views of interviewers' strategies and their own; a study of the relative efficiency of board and sequential interviews; and, implicit in all of these, the value of a counselling skills approach to selection interviewing. Basic counselling skills seem to me to be at the heart of an integrated approach to interviewing, and of the problem of determining its limits as a technique for judging people; but this is more a footprint than a blueprint, more a matter of opinion than evidence, at the moment.

References

1. Eysenck, H. J., *Uses and Abuses of Psychology*, Penguin, Harmondsworth, 1955.
2. Warr, P. B., 'Judgments about people at work', in P. B. Warr (ed.), *Psychology at Work*, Penguin, Harmondsworth, 1971.
3. Anstey, E., *An Introduction to Selection Interviewing*, HMSO, London, 1977.
4. Bayne, R., 'Can selection interviewing be improved?' *Journal of Occupational Psychology*, vol. 50, pp. 161–7, 1977.
5. Grant, D. L. and Bray, D. W., 'Contributions of the interview to assessment of management potential', *Journal of Applied Psychology*, vol. 53, pp. 24–33, 1969.
6. Schmitt, N., 'Social and situational determinants of interview decisions: Implications for the employment interview', *Personnel Psychology*, vol. 29, pp. 79–101, 1976.
7. Arvey, R. D., 'Unfair discrimination in the employment interview: Legal and psychological aspects', *Psychological Bulletin*, vol. 86, pp. 736–65, 1979.
8. Webster, E. C., *Decision-making in the Employment Interview*, Eagle, Montreal, 1964.
9. Randell, G., 'Interviewing at work', in P. B. Warr (ed.), *Psychology at Work*, 2nd edn, Penguin, Harmondsworth, 1979.

10. Hinrichs, J. R., 'Personnel training', in M. D. Dunnette (ed.), *Handbook of Industrial and Organisational Psychology*, Rand McNally, Chicago, 1976.
11. Lewis, C., Edgerton, N. and Parkinson, R., 'Interview training: Finding the facts and minding the feelings', *Personnel Management*, May, 29–33, 1976.
12. Davison, R., 'Training for selection interviewers', *Training Research Bulletin*, vol. 8, pp. 8–12, 1978.
13. Maguire, P., and Rutter, D., 'Training medical students to communicate', in A. E. Bennett (ed.), *Communication between Doctors and Patients*, Oxford University Press, 1976.
14. Argyle, M., *The Psychology of Interpersonal Behaviour*, 3rd edn, Penguin, Harmondsworth, 1978.
15. Wright, D. S., 'Meditating', *The Listener*, vol. 84, pp. 656–8, 1970.
16. Harding, D. E., *The Science of the 1st Person*, Shollond Publications, Ipswich, 1974.
17. Bayne, R., 'Effective listening, interviewer state of consciousness, and a mental exercise', *Personnel Review*, vol. 9, pp. 30–4, 1980.
18. Keenan, A. E. and Wedderburn, A. A. I., 'Putting the boot on the other foot: Candidates' descriptions of interviewers', *Journal of Occupational Psychology*, vol. 53, pp. 81–9, 1980.
19. Fletcher, C., 'Candidates' beliefs and self-presentation strategies in selection interviews', *Personnel Review*, Spring 1981.
20. Bayne, R., Colwell, J. and Fletcher, C., 'An experimental comparison of board and sequential interviewing'. Presented at the Annual Conference of the British Psychological Society, Aberdeen University, 1980. Paper also submitted for publication.
21. Lewis, C., 'Investigating the employment interview: A consideration of counselling skills', *Journal of Occupational Psychology*, vol. 53, pp. 111–16, 1980.
22. Egan, G., *The Skilled Helper*, Brookes/Cole, Monterey, 2nd edn, 1982.
23. Gilmore, S. K., *The Counselor-in-Training*, Prentice-Hall, Englewood Cliffs, NJ, 1973.

6. Perceiving others: The psychology of interpersonal perception

MARK COOK

Psychologists often feel defensive about their science, apologizing profusely for the vagueness and obviousness of their findings; often they have good cause to feel defensive, for they have not anything very startling to say. Fortunately for my self-esteem as an academic psychologist, I do not find myself in that embarrassing position when describing the results of some 100 years of scientific research on the way people form judgements of each other. (I date the scientific study of person perception from Darwin's 1872 book, *Expression of the Emotions in Man and Animals.*) The picture I get from this century's worth of research, of the way people actually form judgements of each other, bears little resemblance to the picture I had before I studied psychology, and hence presumably little resemblance to the picture either layman or expert has. Let me give some structure to my account, by making three 'bold assertions'.

1. Much of the time, people's judgements of each other are wrong.
2. Much of the rest of the time, people's judgements of each other are vague and unverifiable.
3. Most people avoid realizing (1) and (2) by deluding themselves about the way they judge others.

Wrong much of the time

Whenever a person's ability to say what someone thinks, or feels, or intends to do next is put to a proper test, that person's performance barely exceeds chance level. (In experiments, unlike real life, you have to commit yourself to an answer, which is usually yes or no for the experimenter's convenience; hence you are bound to get some of the answers right just by guesswork.)

The layman as judge of others

In a recent piece of research, Dane Archer[1] used his Social Interpretations Test, which consists of short sequences of filmed behaviour, followed by a simple question requiring an unambiguous answer. For example, two women are seen with a child and the question is: which woman is the child's mother? Or two men are seen leaving a tennis court, and the question is: which of the two won the game? Most people probably think they would do fairly well on this test, but Archer's subjects certainly did not. Guesswork would give them 6 out of 16 answers right (some questions had three possible answers); Archer's sample managed to exceed this to the modest extent of just under 9 correct predictions. Several other similar studies have obtained similar results: performances much nearer chance level than full marks.

Fancher[2] presented his judges with biographies of real people, converted into 'programmed case studies', which means that after reading some background material the judge is presented with a critical point in the person's life and asked to say which of several choices he made; e.g., at the outbreak of the Second World War, did he (an American citizen) join the US Marines/ start a master's degree in political science/go to London as a war correspondent? After each prediction, the judge is given the correct answer, so his impression of the person is continuously corrected. In Fancher's study guesswork would achieve an average of 4 correct answers in 12, compared with the 5 or so his judges actually achieved. Presumably most professional judges of others would expect to do rather better than that in interpreting someone's biography.

Other research, some of it done by myself and Jacqueline Smith,[3] has shown that people are rather poor at placing others in order of possession of a particular characteristic, an exercise often undertaken at the end of selection conferences. Teachers can give non-random estimates of their pupils' relative standing in intelligence, and students can do the same for their peers' extraversion; but neither sets of estimates are anywhere near good enough to warrant using them to make important decisions (average correlation between test and estimate being about 0.50 in each case). Attempts to place others in rank order of neurotic tendency generate lists of random numbers; people just cannot do it.

Marriage.   It is a legitimate criticism of academic research in this field that the people judging each other do not really know each other, and have no incentive to make accurate judgements; yet a large body of research of accuracy of person perception before and during marriage suggests this criticism is unfounded. For example, Dymond[4] studied groups of happily and unhappily married couples and found that the former could predict their spouse's answers to 38 of 55 questions, while the latter could manage only 33 right. The difference between the two groups is fairly small, and both scores, once again, are much nearer chance level—27 or 28—than full marks. Numerous other studies find similar results; it is very difficult to show that people who have been together a long time know each other better, or that people who are not happy together see each other more clearly than people who are happy together. (Yet helping the couple see each other's point of view seems a central part of many marriage guidance and therapy programmes.) In fact, what many married couples do much of the time is assume an agreement that is not there; they commonly err in the direction of expecting the other to share an opinion about, for instance, communism or birth control or the role each should take in the family, when in fact he or she does not. This 'assumed similarity' is also found in friends and acquaintances.

Stereotype accuracy.   Research on the way people judge each other also consistently finds that many correct judgements are examples of 'stereotype accuracy'. Asked to say what a particular person will say or do, the judge instead says what people in general would do; and such are the similarities between people, and such is the force of social custom, that this generalized prediction is often right. A frequently cited study by Gage[5] showed that judges' predictions about 'a typical college student' fitted individual students better than judgements that judges made about these same students after seeing them individually. Now, this implies that, if one were interviewing these students, one by one, to decide which of them would make the best management trainee, and if Gage's principle applied, one would be wasting one's time; seeing each individual would not add to what one knew about him or her as a recent college graduate. It emerges from several studies that, when the experimenter changes the task to prevent the judge from making stereotypically accurate judgements, for example, by eliminating all items where most of the people say the same, the judge's ability to make correct predictions is drastically reduced. Perceiving individual differences within a mass of relatively similar people is much more difficult than correctly identifying what the most likely response of the group as a whole will be. Obviously, both skills are useful, but possibly to different people. Stereotype accuracy—being in tune with the man in the street—must be invaluable for advertising men, politicians, and management, but is less useful to the personnel selector, whose task usually is to distinguish between a group of fairly similar applicants.

The self-fulfilling prophecy.   A popular device for making wrong judgements about other people and getting away with it is the self-fulfilling prophecy. An obvious example is the creation of mutual hostility when one person acts on the false impression that another dislikes him. A subtler example of the self-fulfilling prophecy comes from Whyte's[6] classic study of an American street gang, an 'organization' whose main activity was playing bowls, so that it followed that proficiency at bowls and status within the organization were closely linked. Whyte was surprised one day to find that a low-status member of the gang was actually a very good bowls player, but only when away from the rest of the gang; when he was with the gang, barracking and horseplay kept his play down to the level expected of him.

The expert judge of others

College students, married couples, and schoolteachers consistently make inaccurate judgements of each other, often achieving little better than guesswork. Experts might be expected to do better. But they do not: another very consistent finding is that experts, including psychologists, are not better than laymen at predicting what someone will do next. (They are probably better at concealing the fact behind a smokescreen of verbiage, but that point belongs to the next section of this chapter.) Nor, unfortunately, is there much evidence that training or experience improves the quality of judgement significantly. For example, exposure to 'sensitivity training', in which people are encouraged to express their feelings and opinions freely with the aim of increasing interpersonal sensitivity, does not improve one's ability to predict what someone will do or say next (but it does increase the amount of psychological jargon people use).

Psychiatric diagnosis. When one studies the expert on his home ground, he does not fare much better. If a number of psychiatrists see a number of patients, and formulate their diagnoses without comparing notes, they tend to disagree rather frequently. On the major categories of mental illness— psychosis, neurosis, organic brain disorder, character disorder—they agree from 64 to 84 per cent of the time; but when becoming more specific—what type of neurosis, etc.—they agree less well, reaching a low point of 33 per cent agreement. In fairness, one should point out that much of their uncertainty results from an unsatisfactory diagnostic system. Slightly more alarming is the oft-cited study of Rosenhan,[7] who infiltrated volunteers into American psychiatric hospitals with feigned symptoms of mild schizophrenia (hearing a voice saying 'empty', 'hollow', 'thud'): they were duly diagnosed in most cases as schizophrenic; they then stopped feigning any further symptoms and waited to be discovered. It was a long wait; more were detected as not belonging there by their fellow patients than by the hospital staff.

Selection for employment. What of the selection interviewer, and employment selection generally? The picture is much the same. The extensive research has been reviewed several times,[8] and it consistently emerges that selection assessments and performance on the job are only tenuously related. The relation is expressed as a correlation coefficient, which can range from 0.00, meaning that assessment and performance are totally unrelated, to 1.00, meaning a perfect one-to-one correspondence. The correlations between selection assessments and job performance are rarely higher than 0.50, and frequently are below 0.30. Now, a selection process with an accuracy coefficient as good as 0.50 still makes many mistakes. Supposing that half the candidates are accepted; Table 6.1(a) shows that 17 unsuitable candidates would join 33 good ones, while 17 acceptable candidates would be rejected. The lower the selection ratio, the more depressing the picture becomes. If 1 in 5 candidates are to be accepted—perhaps a more likely ratio for better jobs— Table 6.1(b) shows that unsuitable candidates accepted will outnumber the good ones, with a corresponding number of good candidates missed. If the accuracy coefficient is a more modest 0.25 and the selection ratio still 1 in 5, then Table 6.1(c) shows that selection gives such a small margin over sticking a pin in the list—a likely 6 good candidates chosen against 4—that it is hardly cost-effective.

Table 6.1(a) Percentage of good and bad candidates accepted and rejected, where the selection procedure has a validity of 0.50 and half the candidates are accepted

	Good	Bad
Accepted	33	17
Rejected	17	33

Table 6.1(b) Percentage of good and bad candidates accepted and rejected, where the selection procedure has a validity of 0.50 and one-fifth of the candidates are accepted

	Good	Bad
Accepted	9	11
Rejected	11	69

Table 6.1(c) Percentage of good and bad candidates accepted and rejected, where the selection procedure has a validity of 0.25 and one-fifth of the candidates are accepted

	Good	Bad
Accepted	6	14
Rejected	14	66

The two great unknowns.   Accuracy in selection is so poor partly because people just are not very good at judging others, and partly because they will not admit it, but also because there are two great unknowns in the equation. The first unknown is what counts as a successful performance. This depends in most cases on some person's opinion, so one is comparing one set of opinions (the selection team's) with another set (those of the foremen, supervisors, etc.). One supervisor will not agree completely with another supervisor on the merits of their subordinates, so the selection team have the hopeless task of trying to pick someone to suit an uncertain set of requirements. This problem remains whatever criterion of success one employs; none is perfectly reliable, so the selector is always trying to predict the unpredictable.

The second great unknown is the quality of the candidates who were rejected. One has no information about their success at the job, because they were never allowed to try it; this means that one calculates the accuracy of the selection process from a 'restricted range' of candidates. Unless the selection process was entirely useless, it will have succeeded in rejecting some of the obviously unsuitable candidates, but they will not figure in the calculation of the method's accuracy.

These two unknowns in the calculation mean that validity coefficients can never be 1.00 or anywhere near it; it is impossible to have a perfectly accurate selection method, and one should be suspicious of anyone who claims to possess such a thing.

Vague and unverifiable

Some judgements of people are sufficiently specific so that it is easy to check whether they are correct or not. A person does or does not believe in communism; will or will not reject the offer you are about to make; will or will not admit to having frequent nightmares. All these questions are easily verified. But there is a second class of judgements that are much broader and vaguer, are much more difficult to check, and are much more frequently made. When asked to describe someone else, most people use words like 'friendly', 'pleasant', 'materialistic', 'impulsive' (examples chosen from other chapters in this book). Words like this, which say something about a whole range of behaviour, are called 'trait words'. Some apply to limited areas of behaviour— 'motherly', 'punctual'—whereas others cover the whole range of a person's thoughts and actions—'extravert' or 'intelligent'. The number of trait words in the English language is bigger than the average person's entire vocabulary; Allport and Odbert's[9] classic analysis listed 17 953, some admittedly archaic or metaphorical. Psychologists have not been slow to add to the list, and many of their jargon words have won general acceptance—'anal personality', 'cyclo-thymic', 'schizoid', etc.

The value of trait descriptions

A trait word is said to do two things; summarize past behaviour, and predict future behaviour. Having summarized someone's past behaviour—does not donate to Oxfam, sits in the cold, avoids buying a drink when it is his turn, etc.—with a trait label ('mean'), one can then use the label to predict how he will behave on a fresh set of occasions involving parting with money or valuables, and not waste one's breath asking him to lend 50p. Hence, the ability to characterize someone by a suitable choice of trait labels is fundamental in judging people.

Such at any rate is the theory; in practice, traits commonly fail to summarize or predict. One cannot derive any particular prediction from a trait statement. Saying 'Smith is intelligent' covers a vast range of possibilities from his choice of television viewing to his grasp of mathematics, but does not definitely imply any single item; the statements 'Smith is intelligent' and 'Smith can't play chess' are not contradictory: a single exception to a trait statement does not disprove it, any more than a single confirmation proves it.

Nor do traits always summarize past behaviour. People are fairly consistently intelligent across a wide variety of tasks, which is why it is possible to talk of general intelligence, but the same is rarely true of personality traits, where exceptions to the rule are generally so frequent as to make the rule virtually non-existent. The classic example is the trait of honesty, studied by Hartshorne and May[10] in 1928. Hartshorne and May had the idea that 'character'—traits such as honesty and persistence—could be measured like intelligence, and perhaps a 'character quotient' devised. This rather sinister proposal came to nothing because they found virtually no transfer from one test of honesty to another. The child who pocketed apparently 'lost' money did not necessarily lie about his athletic achievement; and the child who lied about athletic achievement did not necessarily cheat on a task that required him to keep his eyes shut. They even found that the child who cribbed from one book did not crib from another. These findings, which have been repeated for a number of other traits, like dependency, conformity, and aggressiveness, show that many trait words do not summarize past behaviour, and are very unlikely to predict future behaviour. In fact, Hartshorne and May's findings imply that it is virtually meaningless to describe someone as honest, unless the circumstances are specified precisely. This in turn implies that being told someone is honest, or dependable, or aggressive, is potentially very misleading, because it is likely that the listener's idea of honesty will not correspond to the speaker's. Oldfield[11] asked a number of people what they understood by 'reliable'; he found some took it to mean predictability— always doing the *same* thing— whereas others included the notion of consistently meeting obligations— always doing the *right* thing. Others gave it more specific interpretations, such as the ability to work without supervision, or even the avoidance of saying things one would later regret. Far from acting as a useful way of summarizing the diversity of an individual's behaviour, the trait statement is often a source of confusion and misunderstanding.

In fact, many trait names convey little more than approval, meaning simply that the describer likes the described: 'good', 'kind', 'fair', 'nice' are all largely, in psychological jargon, expressions of positive evaluation. One suspects that a perusal of selection and appraisal reports would yield a further crop of thinly disguised evaluations.

Verifying trait statements

The point about expressing judgements of others in trait terms is that probably 95 per cent of them are uncheckable. One can therefore make elaborate-sounding judgements of one's fellows with little risk of being proved wrong, and correspondingly little promise of conveying much useful information. Judgements of someone's intelligence can be checked against an intelligence test. Judgements about some aspects of personality can, with considerably less certainty, be checked against personality tests. But judgements about 'maturity' or 'forcefulness' or 'team spirit' cannot be checked against anything, because much of what they refer to is in the mind of the describer, not in the behaviour of the described.

The discussion till now has deliberately been restricted to straightforward trait descriptions; but many judges of others do not limit themselves to simple statements about aggressiveness or anxiety, but go boldly on to give reasons. There is, for example, the old favourite, 'he/she is aggressive because he/she is basically insecure and trying to boost his/her self-confidence'. Or a more ambitious example, from Berg's book, *The Unconscious Significance of Hair*,[12] explaining why some men expose themselves in public:

> The exhibitionist seems to have been concerned not only as to whether the mother would approve or castrate the phallus, but, earlier than this, as to whether she would approve or condemn his faeces. . . . He is suing for his mother's approval and appreciation of what he himself (as a baby) loves and appreciates so much, namely, his faeces, his anal eroticism.

Academic psychologists, like Philip Vernon[13] have pointed out over and over again how difficult it is to prove claims like these. It is also rather hard in many cases to determine their practical relevance for everyday life or work.

The 'Barnum effect'

It has been suggested that people use trait words and 'dynamic' interpretations to give themselves a feeling that they understand other people. There certainly is evidence that people are easily satisfied by being given a description of themselves in trait and dynamic terms. Snyder[14] gave his class a personality test, waited while it was supposedly scored and analysed, then handed every student an assessment of his/her personality. In fact, the same set of all-purpose platitudes (e.g., 'disciplined and controlled on the outside, you tend to be worrisome and insecure on the inside') was in every envelope. The students mostly accepted the descriptions as searching and profound insights into their own individual personalities. Snyder dubbed this the 'Barnum effect', in memory of the circus proprietor's cynical dictum, 'there's one born every minute'. Professional judges of others are always in danger of falling into the Barnum trap, by issuing weighty all-purpose verdicts that apply to nearly everyone.

Perhaps I might end this section with an appeal to logical positivism. The philosopher A. J. Ayer[15] managed, 40 odd years ago, to clear a vast jungle of verbiage by applying the simple rule that, if you cannot specify what set of observations would prove or disprove your statement, it does not mean anything. A dose of logical positivism would not harm most people who pride themselves in being good judges of others.

Common forms of self-delusion about judging people

The argument so far is that, when people commit themselves to saying something definite about other people, they are often wrong, and that much of the time they play safe by making judgements of other people that are essentially unverifiable. The third part of the argument is that people consistently delude themselves about the way they judge others. There may be a causal link between this proposition and the other two; perhaps people are inaccurate and vague because they delude themselves, or perhaps they have to delude themselves to avoid realizing how bad their judgement really is.

Intuition or inference?

Much of the self-delusion centres on the concept of intuition, a faculty unrecognized by scientific psychology but frequently claimed by social workers, personnel men, clinical psychologists, and other experts, and generously attributed to the entire female sex. It also goes under the names 'flair', 'experience', or 'insight', and sometimes finds an anatomical location in the 'eye' or 'nose'. Much the same idea is often expressed by the word 'clinical', as in 'clinical skill', or 'clinical experience'; when people start invoking these, they often mean that they are not prepared to defend or explain their opinion, even if, or especially if, it conflicts with other non-'clinical' evidence.

The academic psychologist is sceptical of all these claims, and wants an analysis of human judgement in terms of what inference is being drawn from which piece(s) of information, and with what degree of validity; indeed, some academic psychologists seek to replace the expert judge of others by a list of items, each with its assigned weight in the final decision.

The 'inference' model sees judging other people, whether in the psychiatric clinic, in the selection conference, or in everyday life, as essentially resembling the thought processes of Sherlock Holmes. You draw an inference from what you can see (and hear, etc.) to what you cannot. You see the double indentation on the lower part of the woman's sleeve, and infer that she is a typist. You observe the reddening of the face, hear the rising of voice, and infer someone is angry. You read the history of absenteeism and under-achievement and infer the applicant will not make a good manager. Some theorists (notably Sarbin[16]) have expressed this view of the way people judge each other in the form of a syllogism; here is a typical example:

All persons with histories of absenteeism and under-achievement make poor managers;
this applicant has such a history;
therefore he will make a poor manager.

Implicit personality theories.   Sarbin *et al.*'s formulation draws attention to the fact that every individual has a set of ideas about people and the way they behave: an 'implicit personality theory' (implicit because its owner may not be able to describe it). A study by Wiggins[17] examined implicit theories about intelligence and its manifestations; they found that two-thirds of their sample thought, correctly, that the best cues (of the nine supplied) to high intelligence were wide vocabulary and good school achievement. About one-third had less accurate ideas, thinking that intelligence went with high social status and hard work at school. A few individuals had bizarre ideas; one thought that the only cue to intelligence was mental stability, and furthermore that the *less* stable the person was the *more* intelligent he would be. Implicit personality theories often include stereotypes—Xs are drunken and stupid, Ys and lazy and super-stitious, Zs are clever but unreliable, where X, Y, and Z are races, nationalities, professions, sexes, etc. Equal opportunity laws have probably forced most professional judges of others to discard some of these stereotypes; I would argue that they should go much further and replace their ideas wherever possible by theories based on fact, and by fact I mean systematic research and follow-up investigations, not personal experience.

Imperfect association.   The syllogistic model has two drawbacks: it tends to limit itself to inferences drawn from one piece of information, and it fails to include the notion of imperfect association. To take the notion of imperfect association first, it is rarely possible (some philosophers would argue, never possible) to say that all X are Y; there are always exceptions to the rule, and when one is dealing with human behaviour, the exceptions are legion. It is rare to be able to say anything more definite than: 'Rather more people who smoke also cough' or 'There is a tendency for intelligence and short-sightedness to go together' (true, apparently, according to the research of Jahoda[18]). Such statements can be given greater precision by means of the correlation coefficient. The layman is not happy with generalizations as guarded as these, and tends either to argue that any single exception to the generalization invalidates the rule—'my grandfather smoked 50 cigarettes a day and lived till he was 90'—or else to convert a very modest correlation between two qualities into a one-to-one correspondence. Yet for the personnel selector it is vital to know how strong the association is between, say, past absenteeism and future absenteeism. If the association is very low, the selector should assign little weight to past absence in reaching his verdict, regardless of his personal opinion of absenteeism. There is abundant evidence from work at the Oregon Research Institute[19] that people cannot think like this, and persist in treating a piece of information as useful long after they have had evidence that its real association with what they are trying to predict is virtually zero.

Intuition.   By now I suspect many readers will be getting impatient, seeing, in talk of 'inferences from available information' and 'imperfectly correlated variables being given less weight', no resemblance to how they normally judge other people. They know they are not little tin Sherlock Holmes noting details of appearance, then drawing on their knowledge of 50 types of cigar ash in order to identify a complete stranger as the King of Bohemia in disguise. Their thought processes do not fit the three-stage model: an implicit personality theory, observed detail, conclusion. My first reply is to ask how else you could form a judgement of someone, except on the basis of what you see, and what you know (or think you know). My second reply is take a closer look at the main rival explanation: intuition.

When the concept of intuition is examined,[20] it turns out to have a number of different meanings, none of which quite resembles what those who boast of the faculty have in mind.

INFALLIBILITY.   Sherlock Holmes is almost always right, but then he is a fictional character; real judges of others are wrong a lot of the time. If the first section of this chapter was not sufficiently convincing, more evidence on the fallibility of human judgement in everyday life is presented in my book *Perceiving Others*, and more on the fallibility of selection interviewers by Ulrich and Trumbo.[21]

INNATENESS. Animals do not have to learn to give or recognize threat displays, but are born with the knowledge 'wired in'; it seems unlikely that such built-in perceptual mechanisms could help the human judge much, especially in areas like personnel selection.

GLOBAL, HOLISTIC OR UNANALYSABLE. People who boast that they rely on intuition argue that their thought processes cannot be analysed. It may be true that they themselves cannot analyse them, but the academic psychologist cannot accept that they are inherently unanalysable, which leads on to the final point.

SPEED. Opinions about others are often reached in minutes—studies of interviewing show the first five minutes to be particularly important—and *can* be reached in seconds. To the perceiver, an instant dislike is just that: instant. So how can all this leisurely Holmesian process of observation–inference–conclusion be going on? First, an instant dislike is not really instantaneous; it takes half a second to recognize someone you know very well, so to recognize a stranger as resembling someone you particularly dislike, or as having some feature you especially hate, must take at least as long. Second, there is plenty of evidence that people can learn to make complicated judgements on a time scale measured in fractions of a second: driving one's car to work requires a continuous succession of complex high-speed decisions. Learning to drive includes learning to make these decisions, and the process is not complete until the driver can make them without conscious thought. If all that people mean by 'intuition' is a skill so thoroughly learned that one is not conscious of its operation, I certainly would not quarrel with that. But if they claim that it is something more, I find it difficult to see what that the 'thing' might be, unless they mean extra sensory perception (ESP). And if they claim that judgements based on intuition are better than predictions made by conscious processes of inference based on information of proven value, then I am afraid the evidence is heavily against them.

Clinical prediction v. the 'cookbook'.

The 'cookbook' The personnel selector has five main types of information at his/her disposal:

- The application form, containing details of qualifications, previous posts, past achievements, etc.
- References and testimonials
- The interview
- Personality and ability test data
- 'Signs', as interpreted by graphologists, astrologers, palmists, etc.

Even if the selection team restrict themselves to the traditional trio of form, references, and interview, they are going to discover a lot of facts about the candidate, and it is unlikely that all these facts will point the same way. Some system of giving each piece of information a weight in the final decision is required, and this immediately leads back to the question of intuition v. conscious inference. The inference method lists every fact, and puts a plus, zero, or minus against it, according to whether it is a good point, an irrelevant point, or a bad point, then adds them up and chooses the candidate(s) with the best score(s). This method may be refined by giving differential weight to certain items, either on the ground that they are more important, or on the ground that they add more fresh information. (If the selection team gave an intelligence test, and a mechanical comprehension (MC) test, they would probably find it better to give the MC test only a fraction of the marks given to the intelligence test, since MC tests also measure general intelligence. Giving both tests full weight might therefore give intelligence too much say in the decision.

A further refinement is a follow-up study to find out how well each fact actually predicts success. This enables the selection team to give each fact exactly the weight it merits, dispense with procedures that do not predict success, and dispense with procedures that do predict success but are redundant. The final step is to convert the information obtained by such a follow-up into a prediction table. The selection team, now reduced to a semi-skilled clerk, check off items on a standard list, give each its assigned weight, and arrive at a number representing the final assessment. This method, called 'statistical' or 'actuarial' prediction, resembles in most ways the calculation of motor insurance premiums, and it has been used to predict re-offending in delinquents and criminals, likelihood of suicide, probable benefit from different types of psychiatric treatment, and suitability for employment as a clinical psychologist, among other purposes.

A paper by Robyn Dawes[22] suggests that, for most practical purposes, the procedure can be simplified to the careful selection of a set of relevant facts, each of which is given exactly the same weight in the decision. The vital point is to include only items that are relevant—relevance meaning having good predictive power, rather than consonance with your private theory of the ideal employee.

The clinical method.   The clinical expert is sceptical of statistical techniques; the essence of his approach, according to Gough,[23] is that 'the combining [of different pieces of information] is done intuitively ... hypotheses and constructs are generated during the course of the analysis ... and the process is mediated by an individual's judgement and reflection'. The clinical expert reaches a conclusion from some or all of the available information, but is not necessarily able to say what cues he uses, or how much weight he attaches to each. The clinical method has strong appeal, because a visible effort is being made to understand the individual; an actuarial table, by contrast, looks inhuman and bureaucratic. Which, then, is better? Should one leave the clinical expert to absorb all the facts, allow them to stew awhile, and await an answer? Or should one start drawing up a checklist of good and bad points? The clinical expert argues that he can interpret the data in ways the table cannot; he can use his experience and knowledge of the person to discount certain points and give greater weight to others. Above all, he can see each fact in the light of the others, so that he responds to the case as a meaningful whole, or 'configuration'. Common sense suggests the clinical expert must be better than the 'cookbook'. And, not surprisingly, the clinical expert is the first to agree.

However, work at the Oregon Research Institute casts doubt on the expert's claim to use information in subtle 'configural' ways; analysis of the way experts used sets of five or six cues to reach decisions about releasing patients,[24] or to diagnose ulcers from X-ray photos,[25] found little evidence that judges used configurations of cues. Most of the time they used their favourite facts, and reached their verdict by adding them up, just like a simple prediction table. In any case, if elaborate 'configural' decisions were needed, flow diagrams or computer programs could be used to work them out automatically. In fact, it appears from the work on parole violation and on psychiatric diagnosis from personality questionnaires that complex decision processes are not really necessary; a simple weighted average gives as good a prediction as any.

Meehl reviewed the merits of the two approaches in his classic study, *Clinical versus Statistical Prediction*[26]; he found that the statistical/actuarial method—the 'cookbook', he dubbed it—was always as good as the clinical expert, and usually better. Subsequent research has consistently confirmed Meehl's original conclusion. The expert cannot do any better than the 'cookbook', nor can he even take the 'cookbook's' prediction as the starting point for a more accurate prediction of his own.

An interesting study by Goldberg[27] tried, in effect, to combine the clinical and statistical methods by analysing the expert's decisions and constructing a set of rules to reproduce the way he thinks. The fascinating point is that this set of rules—'the model of man', as Goldberg calls it—can then do better than the expert it was derived from.

Samples, 'signs', and empirical keying

Four of the five selection methods listed—form, reference, interview, and tests—are essentially samples of the candidate's behaviour. The man who can solve the problems in the intelligence test is presumed to be able to solve the problems he will face in his new post. The man who is nervous and inarticulate in the interview will presumably be nervous and inarticulate when trying to sell the organization's product. (The presumption may well be false, v.i.)

The fifth class of information—handwriting, star-charts, etc.—are 'signs'. One does not employ a graphologist to say whether a candidate's handwriting is legible, or a palmist to say if his fingernails are clean, but rather because handwriting and the hand itself are supposed to reveal, quickly and accurately, important aspects of their owner's whole personality. The interpretations of personality offered by graphologists, etc., in Chapters 7–9 below make this abundantly clear; but are they justified in extrapolating so far from marks on paper, or marks on the hand?

The emphasis of this chapter throughout has been that people should try to use valid information when judging others, information that has been shown by systematic research on a large number of people to predict what you want to know. Many early assessment methods did not work on this principle, and were eventually found wanting; collecting facts because common sense said they were good measures of sales potential, or because your theory of sales ability said they were, did not give good results. Consider these two items, used to predict likelihood of re-conviction, in an early American parole study: (1) prisoner's father served jail sentence; (2) prisoner guilty of assault and battery. One might well think the first irrelevant, and that the second points to a poor outlook; but in fact it is the other way round. (For that matter, common sense might argue very plausibly that young men ought to make safer drivers, because their reflexes are faster, were it not the invariable experience of insurance companies that they are actually rather poor risks.) During the 1920s and 1930s, the first 'empirically keyed' assessment techniques were devised; these were prepared to include any item that could predict, regardless of its logical connection with what was being predicted. If a desire to play tiddley-winks after tea on Sunday reliably predicted homicidal mania, then it would be included in the Homicidal Mania Scale. Similarly if handwriting, or instant of birth, or cube root of the distance of birthplace from the Great Pyramids, were reliable signs of management potential, by all means use them. The evidence on astrology, graphology, and palmistry is summarized in other chapters, but it has generally been found in empirically keyed tests that subtle, non-obvious items are the exception. Tests of psychopathic tendency—the nearest thing to a Homicidal Mania Scale—consists largely of expressions of indifference to others' feelings and fondness for causing damage and pain. It is also true that psychological tests that use the 'sign' approach, like the Rorschach inkblot test, neither are particularly reliable nor have much predictive power.

Concluding comment

The model of human judgement recommended in this chapter may seem cold and mechanical; it is meant to be. There is, no doubt, much more to understanding other people than being able to predict what they are going to do next. Understanding, and sympathizing with, another person's character, aspirations, conflicts, doubts, and worries seems a much grander and more worthwhile exercise. But I have stuck closely to a basic making-inferences-from-cues-of-proven-validity model, for two reasons. The first is simply that I suspect it is what is needed in industrial psychology. Second, I have doubts, expressed in the section beginning on page 72, about just what people are really doing when they start producing rounded descriptions of whole personalities. At least, if one sticks just to trying to guess what the other man is going to do next, one will know if one is right or not.

References

1. Archer, D. and Akert, R. M., 'Words and everything else: verbal and non-verbal cues in social interpretation', *Journal of Personality and Social Psychology*, vol. 35, pp. 443–9, 1977.
2. Fancher, R. E., 'Accuracy versus validity in person perception', *Journal of Consulting Psychology*, vol. 31, pp. 264–7, 1967.
3. Cook, M. and Smith, J. S., 'Group ranking techniques in the study of the accuracy of person perception', *British Journal of Psychology*, vol. 65, 427–35, 1974.
4. Dymond, R. F., 'Interpersonal perception and marital happiness', *Canadian Journal of Psychology*, vol. 8, pp. 164–71, 1954.
5. Gage, N. L., 'Judging interests from expressive behavior', *Psychological Monographs*, vol. 66, no. 18 (whole no. 602), 1952.
6. Whyte, W. F., *Street Corner Society: The Social Structure of an Italian Slum*, University of Chicago Press, 1943.
7. Rosenhan, D. L., 'On being sane in insane places', *Science*, vol. 179, pp. 250–8, 1973.
8. Mayfield, E. C., 'The selection interview: A re-evaluation of published research', *Personnel Psychology*, vol. 17, pp. 239–60, 1964; Ulrich, L. and Trumbo, D., 'The selection interview since 1949', *Psychological Bulletin*, vol. 63, 100–16, 1965; Wright, O. R., 'Summary of research on the selection interview since 1964', *Personnel Psychology*, vol. 22, pp. 391–413, 1969.
9. Allport, G. W. and Odbert, S., 'Trait-names: a psycholexical study', *Psychological Monographs*, vol. 47, no. 1 (whole no. 211), 1936.
10. Hartshorne, H. and May, M. A., *Studies in Deceit*, Macmillan, New York, 1928.
11. Oldfield, R. C., 'Some verbal problems connected with character nomenclature', *Journal of Mental Science*, vol. 83, pp. 245–55, 1939.
12. Berg, C., *The Unconscious Significance of Hair*. Allen & Unwin, London, 1951.
13. Vernon, P. E., *Personality Assessment*, Methuen, London, 1964.
14. Snyder, C. R. and Larson, G. R., 'A further look at student acceptance of general personality interpretations', *Journal of Consulting and Clinical Psychology*, vol. 38, pp. 384–88, 1972.
15. Ayer, A. J., *Language, Truth and Logic*, Gollancz, London, 1936.
16. Sarbin, T. R., Taft, R. and Bailey, D. E., *Clinical Inference and Cognitive Theory*, Holt, Rinehart & Winston, New York, 1960.
17. Wiggins, N., Hoffman, P. J. and Taber, T. 'Types of judges and cue utilisation in judgements of intelligence', *Journal of Personality and Social Psychology*, vol. 12, pp. 52–9, 1969.
18. Jahoda, G., 'Refractive errors, intelligence and social mobility', *British Journal of Social and Clinical Psychology*, vol. 1, pp. 96–106, 1963.
19. Kahneman, D. and Tversky, A., 'On the psychology of prediction', *Psychological Review*, vol. 80, pp. 237–51, 1973.
20. Cook, M., *Perceiving Others: The Psychology of Interpersonal Perception*, Methuen, London, 1979; Sarbin *et al.*, *op. cit.*
21. Ulrich and Trumbo, *op. cit.*
22. Dawes, R. M. and Corrigan, B., 'Linear models in decision-making', *Psychological Bulletin*, vol. 81, pp. 95–106, 1974.
23. Gough, H. G., 'Clinical vs statistical prediction in psychology', in L. Postman (ed.), *Psychology in the Making*, Alfred Knopf, New York, 1962.
24. Rorer, L. G., Hoffman, P. J., Dickman, H. R. and Slovic, P., 'Configural judgements revealed', *Proceedings of the Annual Convention of the American Psychological Association*, APA, Washington DC, 1967.
25. Hoffman, P. J., Slovic, P. and Rorer, L. G., 'An analysis of variance model for the assessment of configural cue utilisation in clinical judgement', *Psychological Bulletin*, vol. 69, pp. 338–49, 1968.

26. Meehl, P. E., *Clinical versus Statistical Prediction*, University of Minnesota Press, Minneapolis, 1954.
27. Goldberg, L. R., 'Man versus model of man: a rationale, plus some evidence, for a method of improving clinical inference', *Psychological Bulletin*, vol. 73, pp. 422–32, 1970.

7. Handwriting as a guide to character

KATE LOEWENTHAL

You are a personnel manager sorting through 40-odd letters of application for one particular job, trying to produce a short-list of suitable candidates for interview. Obviously, your choice is going to be largely governed by the relevant skills, qualifications, and experience of the various applicants; but you know that you are going to be left with a number of technically suitable people, all very likely competent to cope with the job. At the back of your mind is the question: is he/she going to be good to work with? You want to know what each person is like and, whether you mean to or not, you are forming impressions of each person from the moment you get any shreds of information. What each person says, how he says it, even the handwriting in front of you: all this contributes to the idea that is willy-nilly taking shape in your mind.

The evidence suggests that people agree quite closely about the characteristics of the authors of handwriting samples. There seem to be widespread stereotypes about what certain handwriting features mean. But are these valid? How well do the various features of handwriting relate to other expressions of personality, and to other behaviour? Is a person with huge, untidy writing likely to be disorganized? When people write, are they aware of the impressions conveyed by their handwriting? How well does the personality expressed by handwriting relate to the person as he sees himself, and as others see him? Would it be a good investment of effort to pay more scrupulous attention to handwriting as a guide to the character and future behaviour of a person?

Graphology, the art—or science—of deducing character from handwriting, occupies an ambivalent place in the public mind. We are all fascinated by bold assertions to the effect that backward-sloping writing indicates an inhibited personality, and the like. We might be attracted by the idea that, armed with a knowledge of simple diagnostic signs such as direction and extent of handwriting slope, spacing, and relative size of upper, middle, and lower parts of letters, we could read the inner secrets of people's minds, amuse our friends, and flatter ourselves with inevitably partly accurate character portraits. But we are also sceptical. Graphological claims have been the subject of reputable scientific scrutiny for decades, and the conclusion of 50 years of scientific investigation is one of only heavily qualified support for certain sophisticated forms of graphoanalysis.

The single-feature approach

A recent book on graphoanalysis claimed to instruct its readers in the ability to recognize their children's inner feelings through their handwriting and drawings. Among the impressive list of traits that can be spotted graphologically are causes of non-learning, resistance to authority, fear of failure, concentration, guilt, and (all-inclusively) temperament. I am inclined to quail when confronted with claims of this magnitude. The efforts of psychologists to establish the validity of such claims might seem puny when contrasted with their size. Over the past 50 years, dozens of studies have looked at the strength of the relationship between aspects of handwriting—including judgements of personality derived from handwriting—and assessments of personality and behaviour of the writers.

The simplest kind of investigation involves single features of handwriting and assessments of single aspects of personality. These investigations have not yielded much by way of positive findings. For instance, Vine[1] examined two aspects of personality which can be easily assessed in a five-minute paper-and-pencil test: introversion—extraversion and neuroticism—stability. Twelve students took this test and produced samples of handwriting. The handwriting samples were given to over 60 judges, and although they agreed well with each other about how introverted and neurotic the author of a given sample was, their judgements did not relate reliably to the personality test measure of these traits. In another study,[2] introversion and neuroticism were measured using the same test, and three features of handwriting were measured: line slope, letter slant, and letter width. There were no reliable associations between the handwriting features and the personality measures. A recent review[3] concluded that in general there is little relationship between single graphic features and assessments of personality. The same conclusion was reached in 1933 by Allport and Vernon in their classic, *Studies in Expressive Movement*,[4] but the message still does not seem to be believed. Popularized graphology is still telling us to the contrary. One of the most colourful examples is the claim that dishonest characters tend not to close the bottoms of rounded letters (a, o, d, etc.). The eminent graphologist Dr Saudek[5] supported this claim by observing that the signatures of 30 per cent of 'habitual thieves of both sexes' in the files of the French police show this symptom. Dr Saudek made some good attempts to get empirical support for his claims for graphoanalysis, so this particular claim may still prove justified. Psychologists are certainly still pursuing the elusive goal that somewhere, sometimes, a simple graphic indicator of some feature of personality will be discovered. Psychological journals are still publishing investigations of this kind: the most recent include an attempt to use writing pressure as an index of aggression, and another to assess, from handwriting, inclinations to commit suicide. One of the most hopeful lines of investigation lies in attempts to establish a relationship between the size of a person's signature and feelings of success, dominance, and self-esteem.

There is one simple feature that we seem to be able to use with considerable validity, and this may encourage hope. The sex of the author of a piece of handwriting can usually be told with above-chance success. Figure 7.1 (page 86) shows some examples. The main clue to identifying sex seems to be simple—circularity—though perhaps characteristics of men's and women's handwriting vary from country to country and from time to time.

An interesting sideline on this area of investigation is the attempt to investigate the characteristics of 'sex-deviant' handwriters: the minority of men who produce feminine-seeming handwriting and of women whose writing seems masculine. Figure 7.1 shows an example of the latter kind. One might be tempted to think that sex-deviant handwriting betrays some sort of character instability (neurosis), or possibly homosexual leanings. But neither of these possibilities seems to be true.[6]

Usually, handwriting is a good guide to sex, but it is hard to think of situations where this would be really useful. Otherwise, single features of handwriting reveal very little about the person.

The 'total' approach

The story changes when we consider the more complex levels of analysis. With the introduction of computers, statistical analysis has moved from the simple correlation of two variables to complex forms of multivariate analysis, in which the interrelations of large numbers of variables can be studied. Operations that would have taken months or years of paper and pencil calculation can be disposed of in a few moments of computer time. This makes it possible to see how combinations of handwriting features relate to personality. Some positive results have been obtained using this approach.[7] In one study,[8] 11 features of handwriting were scored, such as height and breadth of the middle, upper, and lower zones of letters, margin breadth, spacing, and slant. A multivariate analysis revealed three distinct styles, each composed of particular combinations of handwriting features. These three styles reflected the personality traits of extraversion, introversion, and reflectivity (cautiousness).

Combinations of features, rather than single features, may be informative; this may be a reason why, on balance, expert graphologists have given somewhat more accurate identifications and personality assessments on the basis of handwriting than have untrained amateurs.[4] Experts presumably know better what combinations of features to look for, and are less likely to be misled by one single, superficially dominating, feature.

Allport and Vernon[4] studied a variety of expressive movements, including handwriting, voice recordings, and simple drawings. They concluded, wisely, that expressive movement is patterned in complex ways, as is personality, and that the most reliable and valid forms of handwriting analysis are those that

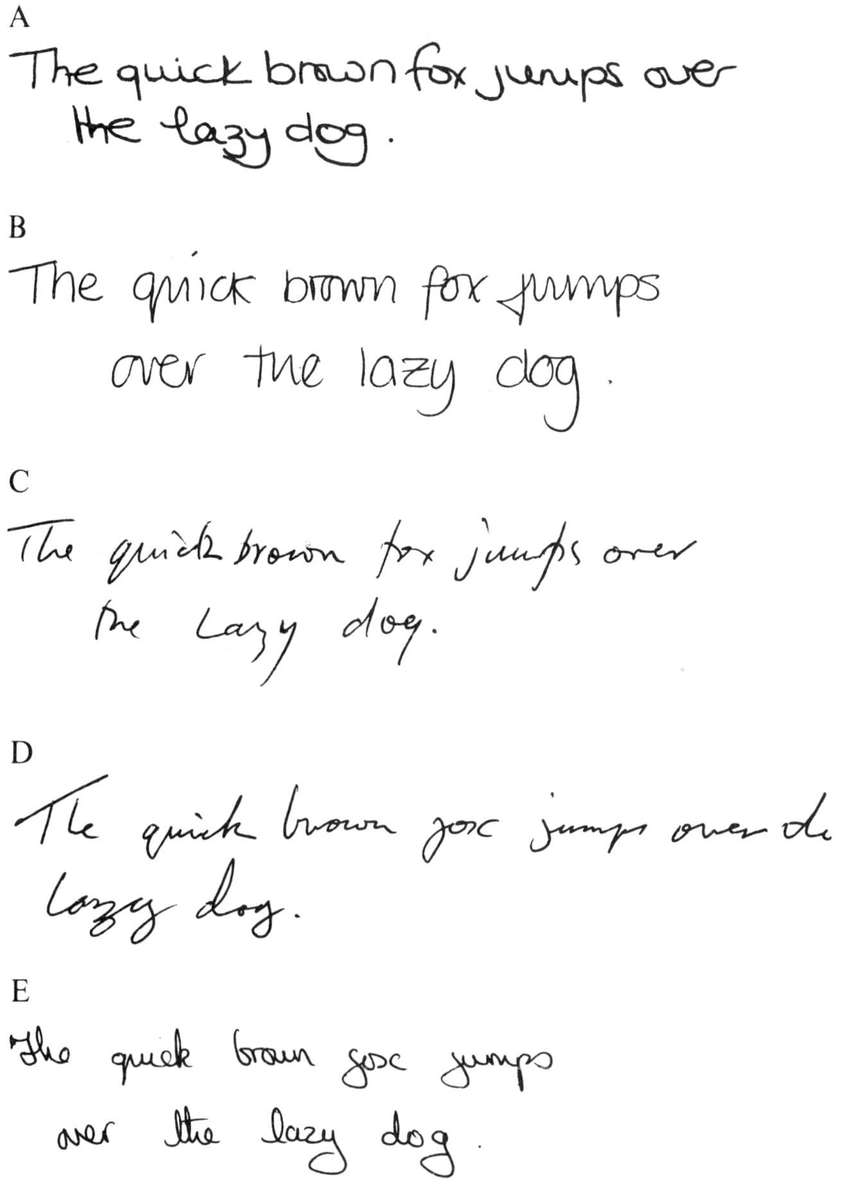

A

The quick brown fox jumps over the lazy dog.

B

The quick brown fox jumps over the lazy dog.

C

The quick brown fox jumps over the lazy dog.

D

The quick brown fox jumps over the lazy dog.

E

The quick brown fox jumps over the lazy dog.

Figure 7.1 A and B are usually correctly identified as women's handwriting, C and D as men's. E is an example of 'sex-deviant' handwriting: though a woman's, it is usually identified as a man's.

adopt a total, holistic approach, examining the handwriting-as-a-whole and personality-as-a-whole. For instance, Fig. 7.2 shows four handwriting samples collected by Allport and Vernon, together with pressure curves taken while the writers were drawing a series of half-inch parallel lines. Allport and Vernon composed thumbnail personality sketches which gave an overall feel of the dominant features of character of the writers of the samples—far more helpful, for most purposes, than a list of scores on personality tests. The reader can try to guess which personality goes with which handwriting (see page 88):

(a) Highly artistic, hyper-active, generous and cheerful, Bohemian
(b) Colourless, quiet, agreeable, and dependable student
(c) Immature, self-assertive, extravagant, unstable second-year student
(d) Forceful, active, efficient businessman, but cautious and exact

The most common error is to mismatch (a) with 3 and (c) with 2; both (a) and (c) are suggested by their personality sketches as being uninhibited and expansive natures, and samples 2 and 3 look far more indicative of this than 1 and 4. The correct matches are: (a)–2, (b)–4, (c)–3, (d)–1. Allport and Vernon's subjects were more likely to make correct matches than incorrect, and expert graphologists were generally better than untrained people. Allport and Vernon were clearly impressed by the often very perceptive judgements made by graphologists.

Figure 7.3 shows an example of handwriting in Hebrew by a distinguished rabbi and communal leader. A graphoanalysis of this handwriting by a graphologist who apparently knew nothing about the writer corresponded closely with features of the writer's personality and philosophy as given in biography, in contemporary anecdotes, and as expressed in his writings. The graphoanalysis includes a discussion of the writer's urge to perceive the unity in existence (he was in fact a noted mystic) and his feeling of responsibility to society (he was active in social welfare work and in political intervention). It is notable that the graphologist had no knowledge of Hebrew and therefore could not have been influenced by the content of what was written.

There is some support for graphology, but many reservations must be made. It is clear that some popularized forms of graphology, which claim that character can be discovered from a simple set of diagnostic signs, have no real basis. More sophisticated forms of graphology, involving more complex analyses of handwriting, may give reliable and sometimes impressive results, but graphology demands lengthy training and probably some talent. A few universities offer courses, and the International Graphoanalysis Society in Chicago offers a three-year training programme. Some graphologists train by serving a fairly lengthy supervised apprenticeship. Dabbling in it would not seem worth while.

Handwriting stereotypes

On the whole, the impressions that people give via their handwriting do not relate closely to measures of their personality. But handwriting does give an

Figure 7.2   Handwriting and pressure curves for four subjects

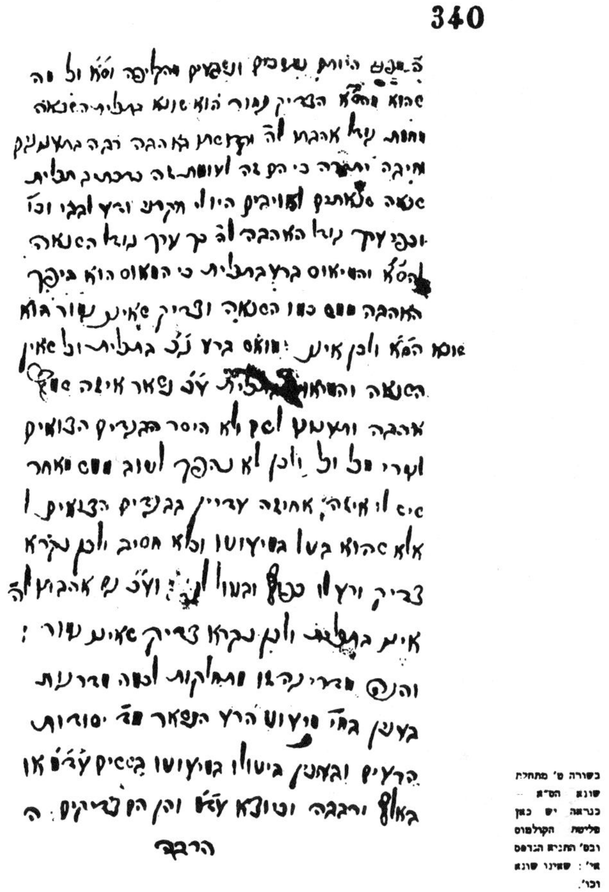
340
בשורה ט' מתחלת
שונא הס"א --
כנראה יש כאן
פליטת הקולמוס
ובס' התניא הנדפס
אי': שאינו שונא
וכו'.

Figure 7.3 The handwriting of Rabbi Schneur Zalman of Liadi (1745–1813)

impression of the writer's personality that is consistently read by other people (even though this reading is not usually very accurate).

The fact that handwriting seems to give a strong impression should not surprise us. Our clothes, appearance, mannerisms, walk—everything about us—is used by other people in forming and modifying their opinions about us. We are often aware of this, and may deliberately exploit different aspects of our appearance and behaviour to communicate different and, we hope, appropriate and useful impressions to other people. We should be embarrassed if forced to dress, for instance, in an unsuitable way. Similarly, we should feel uncomfortable if forced to write in a way that would give a wrong impression of our personality.

In Vine's study mentioned earlier,[1] the 63 student judges were in good agreement about how neurotic and introverted the authors of handwriting samples were, even though their judgements did not relate well to personality test assessments of the writers. Another study[9] found good inter-judge agreement over the traits self-consciousness, stubbornness, persistence, domineering, and attention to detail; the judges in this study were graphologists. I asked teachers and lecturers to assess students' handwriting samples for traits that are important in academic assessment. There was good agreement on the traits clear-thinking, methodical, and original.[10] One wonders how much influence handwriting has in the assessment of examinations and essays. A salutary partial answer to this question is given in a study by Markham,[11] which found that essays in 'better' handwriting were given higher marks by teachers regardless of the quality of the content of the essays.

It seems that we are all unconscious graphologists, making character assessments from handwriting, and agreeing with each other about what a particular specimen means. But our assumptions are unlikely to be very accurate.

Handwriting and self-assessment

I have been rather negative about the relationship—or lack of relationship— between handwriting and personality as assessed by personality tests and other quantified measures. The cynic who has any knowledge of the personality tests used by psychologists might well say that this does not cast so much doubt on the reputation of graphology as on the reputation of psychometrics (the assessment of personality by means of standardized tests). Personality testing is beset by many problems; not the least of these—in the view of the layman who has to take a test—is the apparently ridiculous nature of the questions and tasks that constitute personality tests. It is difficult to give a simple yes or no answer to many questions. What, for example, has what one can see in an ink-blot, or whether one approves of the teaching of Latin, to do with what I am like as a person? This is not the place for a lengthy discussion about the pros and cons of psychometrics; but objections to personality tests do suggest an alternative approach to studying the validity of graphoanalysis.

I have already suggested that handwriting can give a reliable impression of the author, even though the impression is not very accurate when personality tests are used as yardsticks. But perhaps these tests are the wrong yardsticks. Perhaps the impressions given by handwriting are partly or wholly intended by the author, and the personality conveyed resembles the one that the author feels himself to possess, or would like to possess (and this may not relate to personality as psychometrically assessed). This possibility has been tested[10] by getting students to rate themselves on several dimensions thought to be relevant to academic success: clear-thinking, methodical, nervous, original, hard-working. The students rated self (myself as I usually am), ideal self (myself as I should like to be), private social self (myself as I think those close to me see me), and public social self (myself as I think the world in general sees me). Teachers and lecturers rated the students on the five dimensions, solely on the basis of their handwriting. There was no consistent relationship between any of the kinds of self-perception and the handwriting-based assessments of personality. A stronger relationship might be found using a more global level of analysis, but I know of no study of this kind. However, there was evidence that the students felt that they were giving information about themselves (as they saw themselves) via handwriting.

In the study just mentioned, normal handwriting was studied. The same students were also asked to provide samples of their 'best' handwriting, 'as if applying for a job'. With the 'best' handwriting the correlations between self-assessments and personality assessed from handwriting became lower where positive, and more strongly negative when they had originally been negative. This was a consistent effect, and it looked as if the students were deliberately trying to conceal information about themselves. Perhaps this was because they were showing how they would try to create a favourable impression via handwriting, or because they were showing how they give information to strangers: in such a situation there is a tendency to freeze and to withhold personal information until the situation has been tested.

Figure 7.4 shows some examples. The reader might consider whether, when producing best handwriting, the students were deliberately trying to create a good impression, or were deliberately trying to give as slight an impression of themselves as possible.

We have then some indirect evidence that people may use handwriting as a vehicle for self-presentation, or as a means of self-concealment.

The variability of handwriting

Handwriting varies from time to time. Some people are more variable than others, and I do not know whether variability relates to personality. But this fact of variability does illustrate some interesting points.

In spite of variations, handwriting can usually be identified correctly as coming from a particular individual. Figure 7.5 shows two pairs of handwriting samples. On the left is the writing of the preferred, right, hand, on the right that of the non-preferred hand. Incidentally, left-handers generally seem to produce much better controlled writing from their non-preferred hand than do right-handers.

There are superficial dissimilarities, sometimes quite large, but on close inspection it is usually possible to say which pairs of handwriting come from the same person. There are some people who, sadly, because of disablement, must use mouth or feet to write with; and yet, regardless of the limb used to guide the pen, a given individual produces writing that is characteristically his. Handwriting is not so much handwriting as brain-writing.

Normal handwriting varies, sometimes voluntarily, sometimes involuntarily. As well as the common example of 'best' handwriting, voluntary variations include deliberate attempts to disguise, sometimes for sinister purposes. Forensic handwriting experts have achieved some reputation for being able to detect forgeries. People can also produce false impressions of personality via handwriting.[10] Students who were asked to fake the handwriting of methodical and original people produced samples that were reliably judged as such (Fig. 7.6).

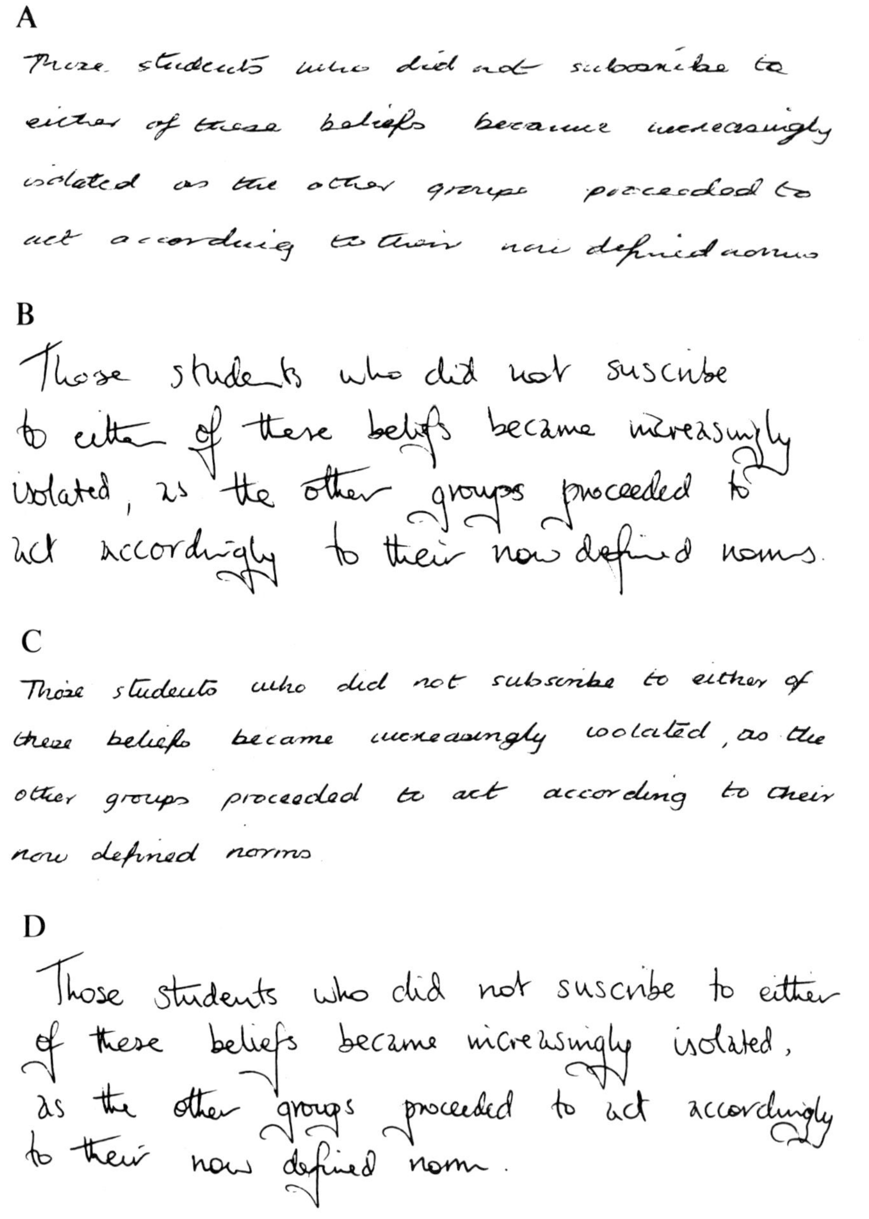

A

Those students who did not subscribe to either of these beliefs became increasingly isolated as the other groups proceeded to act according to their now defined norms

B

Those students who did not suscribe to either of these beliefs became increasingly isolated, as the other groups proceeded to act accordingly to their now defined norms.

C

Those students who did not subscribe to either of these beliefs became increasingly isolated, as the other groups proceeded to act according to their now defined norms

D

Those students who did not suscribe to either of these beliefs became increasingly isolated, as the other groups proceeded to act accordingly to their now defined norm.

Figure 7.4   A and B are samples of normal handwriting, C and D the best handwriting of the same two people.

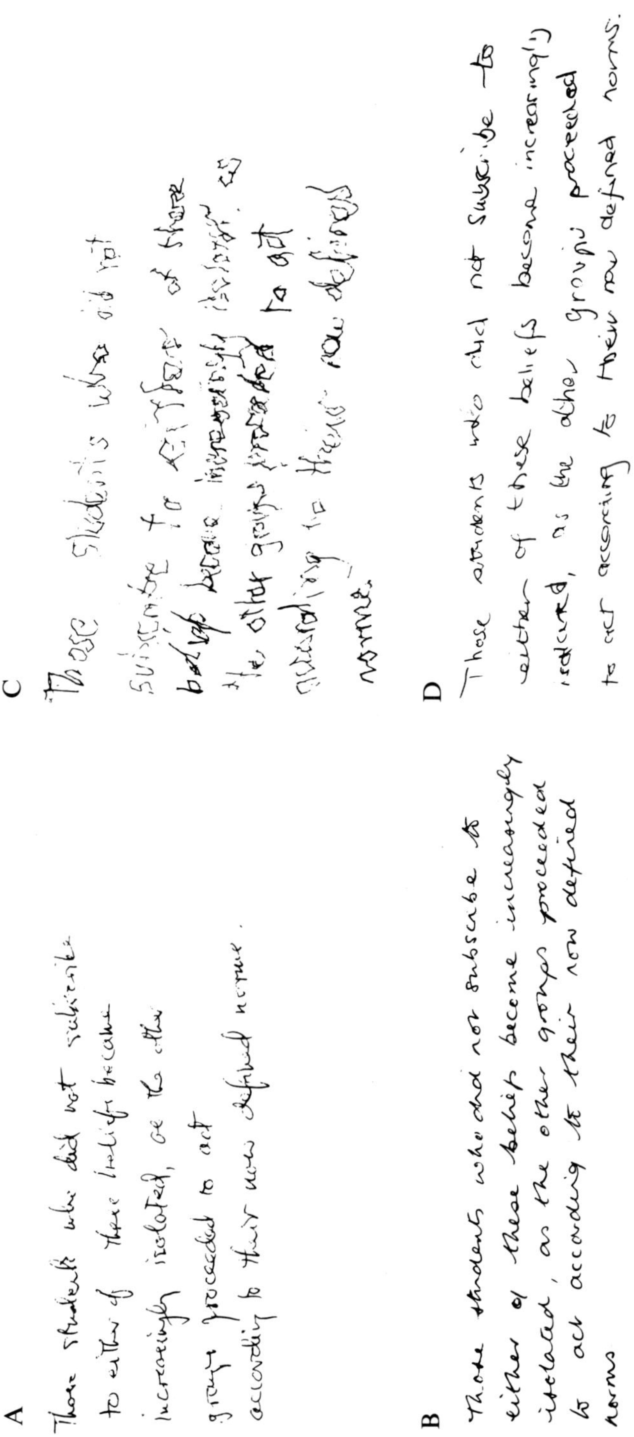

A

Those students who did not subscribe to either of these beliefs became increasingly isolated, as the other groups proceeded to act according to their new defined norms.

B

Those students who did not subscribe to either of these beliefs became increasingly isolated, as the other groups proceeded to act according to their new defined norms

C

Those students who did not subscribe to either of these beliefs became increasingly isolated, as the other groups proceeded to act according to their new defined norms.

D

Those students who did not subscribe to either of these beliefs became increasingly isolated, as the other groups proceeded to act according to their new defined norms.

Figure 7.5   Examples of preferred and non-preferred handwriting by two different people (both are right-handers)

We are thus able to alter our handwriting to produce impressions that may be misleading.

There are variations in handwriting that are clearly involuntary. Downey[12] observed fluctuations in slant, alignment, and total graphic movement that seemed to relate to variations in mood and health, though not always very clearly. A more predictable cause of variation was observed by Wing and Baddeley.[13] They tested a group of people who had spent an evening drinking socially and found reliable differences between the writing of mildly inebriated and sober individuals: for instance, the former produced larger letter 'o's than the latter. The mind boggles slightly at the idea that this might be seized upon as a new cheap substitute for the breathalyser!

The fact that an individual's handwriting is recognizably his or hers, in spite of variations, is of course the source of the fascinating speculations that have surrounded handwriting. Handwriting is stamped with individual characteristics and ought to tell us something about the individual. We have seen that it does tell us a great deal, but that the accuracy of this information is questionable.

How does handwriting compare with other sources of information about people?

There are many settings in which it is important to make an assessment of personality, of habitual ways of behaving and feeling. In assessing people for jobs and for training, in trying to solve educational, social, and psychiatric problems, personality assessment is widely practised. The critics of psychometrics may argue that it has been abused, but it does not seem that we would be on much safer ground with graphology. In certain forms of police work the handwriting expert may be irreplaceable, but in most situations it looks as if interviews and tests will remain popular for a long time. Graphology requires special training and maybe special talent; graphoanalysis is probably an expensive way of making a personality assessment. Similar information could be collected more easily and cheaply by other means. Some firms use graphoanalysis in addition to interviews and tests, so as to collect as wide a range of information as possible.

Dzida and Keiner[14] found that judgements of introversion, intelligence, and aggression were made more reliably and accurately when based on the sound of people's voices and on the way they walked than when based on handwriting and photographs. Most people concerned with occupational selection would feel unhappy about engaging someone they have never met. Whatever its demerits, the conventional face-to-face interview *feels* the safest way of finding out what someone is like.

Summary and conclusions

Single features of handwriting are not reliable indicators of personality, except that circularity is often a reliable indicator of sex. Complex combinations of

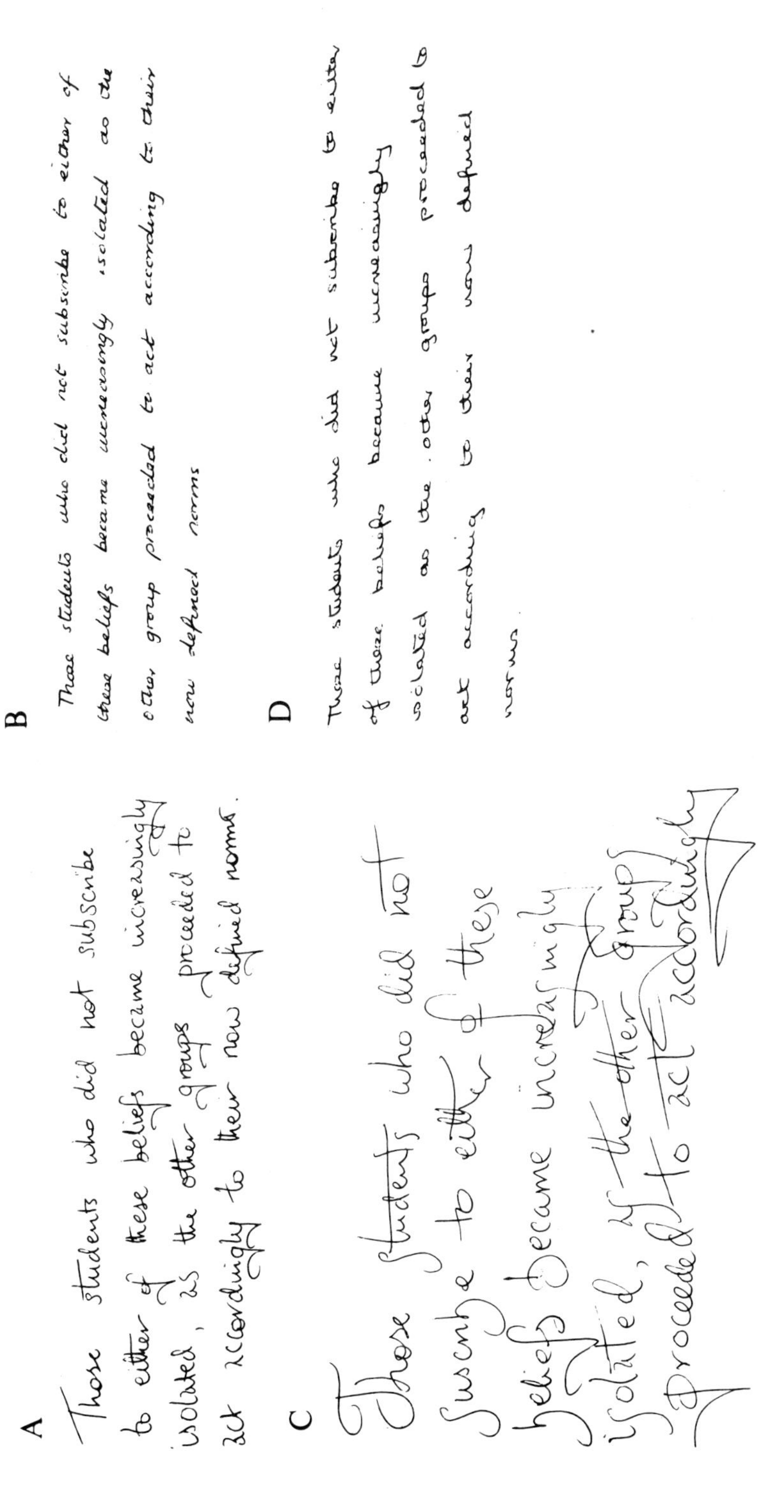

A

Those students who did not subscribe
to either of these beliefs became increasingly
isolated, as the other groups proceeded to
act accordingly to their new defined norms.

B

These students who did not subscribe to either of
these beliefs became increasingly isolated as the
other group proceeded to act according to their
new defined norms

C

Those students who did not
subscribe to either of these
beliefs became increasingly
isolated, as the other group
proceeded to act accordingly

D

These students who did not subscribe to either
of those beliefs because increasingly
isolated as the other groups proceeded to
act according to their new defined
norms

Figure 7.6   A and B are faked methodical handwriting, C and D faked original handwriting. The authors' normal handwriting is shown in Fig. 7.4

handwriting features may be more reliable indicators of personality. Handwriting analysis gives best results when the level of analysis is holistic and when it is done by expert graphologists.

People do agree quite well with each other about the personality impressions conveyed by handwriting, but these impressions are not very accurate. There is some evidence that handwriting may be used as a means of self-presentation.

One should, therefore, beware of one's own amateur attempts to read character from handwriting. Possibly the greatest danger is that these 'attempts' are largely unconscious. Professional graphology may give better results, but it is not wholly reliable; there are probably cheaper and more valid methods of personality assessment to suit most contingencies.

References

1. Vine, I., 'Stereotypes in the judgment of personality from handwriting,' *British Journal of Social and Clinical Psychology*, vol. 13, 1974.
2. Rosenthal, D. and Lines, R., 'Handwriting as a measure of extraversion', *Journal of Personality Assessment*, vol. 42, 1978.
3. Lothar, M., 'Empirical investigations concerning the question of validity and consistency of assessing intellectual levels from handwriting', *Archiv fur die gesamte Psychlogie*, vol. 121, p. 1, 1969.
4. Allport, G. W. and Vernon, P. E., *Studies in Expressive Movement*, Macmillan, New York, 1933.
5. Saudek, R., *The Psychology of Handwriting*, Allen & Unwin, London, 1925.
6. Lester, D., McLaughlin, S., Cohen, R. and Dunn, L., 'Sex-deviant handwriting, femininity and homosexuality', *Perceptual and Motor Skills*, vol. 45, p. 3, 1977.
7. Lemke, E. and Kirchner, J. H., 'A multivariate study of handwriting, intelligence and personality correlates', *Journal of Personality Assessment*, vol. 35, p. 6, 1971.
8. Williams, M., Berg-Cross, G. and Berg-Cross, L., 'Handwriting—extraversion—introversion and Kagan's impulsivity—reflectivity', *Journal of Personality Assessment*, vol. 41, 1977.
9. Galbraith, D. and Wilson, W., 'Reliability of the graphoanalytic approach to handwriting analysis', *Perceptual and Motor Skills*, vol. 19, p. 2, 1964.
10. Loewenthal, K., 'Handwriting and self-presentation', *Journal of Social Psychology*, vol. 96, 1975.
11. Markham, L. R., 'Influence of handwriting quality on teacher evaluation of written work', *American Education Research Journal*, vol. 13, 1976.
12. Downey, J. E., *Graphology and the Psychology of Handwriting*, Warwick and York, Baltimore, 1919.
13. Wing, A. M. and Baddeley, A. D., 'A simple measure of handwriting as an index of stress', *Bulletin of the Psychonomic Society*, vol. 11, 1978.
14. Dzida, W. and Keiner, F., 'Strategies of using nonverbal information in judging personality characteristics', *Zeitschrift fur Experimentelle und Angewandte Psychologie*, vol. 25, 1978.

Acknowledgement

This chapter is a revised and expanded version of an article that appeared in *New Society*, 13 March 1980.

8. Applied astrology: An intuitive approach

SHEILA MACLEOD

Beliefs

There are many speculations about the origin and development of astrology. These include the belief that it was an ancient doctrine that made its way from Atlantis to Egypt, China, India, and the lost civilizations of South America. Another, more practical, suggestion is that it evolved from observations of celestial phenomena and the study of how these correlated with events on earth: the times for sowing and reaping, the times of peace and war, the births and deaths of kings and princes. Over aeons of time this developed into a system of interpreting planetary motions as they relate to the earth in terms of human behaviour and characteristics. In this respect it is as scientific as weather forecasting.

In this chapter I shall be taking an intuitive approach to astrology, and I leave it to the scientists to explain the effects of cosmic influences on living organisms.

The more I work with astrology, the more I become aware that there is a mystery. None of the explanations of how and why it works seems entirely satisfactory. My own approach is to follow a path taken by Carl Jung,[1] who stated that 'Whatever is born, or done, in this moment of time, has the qualities of this moment in time.' The energies and principles symbolized by the planets and signs of the zodiac appear to respond to some acausal connecting principle (synchronicity) and then manifest themselves as human characteristics, behaviour, and life events.

Astrology today

Astrology is currently being used in many different ways. From the world of 'pop' astrology in newspapers and magazines, we move to the use of astrology for birth control which was pioneered in Czechoslovakia by Dr Eugen Jonas.

Although Dr Jonas's astrological birth control clinic is now closed, his methods for controlling fertility, viability, and the sex of unborn children through calculations based on the woman's horoscope are available in a book by Sheila Ostrander and Lynn Schroeder.[2]

My own interest lies in the use of astrology as a method of self-judgement and personal growth. Once we gain a deeper knowledge and insight into ourselves, we are better able to understand the motivation and behaviour of others. As this personal insight grows, a harmony of inner energies develops which makes it possible to become what one has always potentially been capable of being. In practical terms, astrology can be used in conjunction with therapeutic techniques, such as active imagination, to help resolve deep inner conflicts which often need the help of the psychotherapist; it can give an individual an understanding of the dynamics of interpersonal relationships; and it can show each one of us how to optimize the potential that so often lies dormant, or even crippled, because we have drifted into, or been forced into, the wrong type of work occupation or personal relationship.

This chapter looks at how astrological assessment could be used at work. When I had management responsibilities for people, I used the 'approved' methods of judgement with which most managers are familiar. None of the techniques described have been used by any of the organizations for which I have worked. In fact, I am glad that, when astrology first caught my enthusiasm, I was no longer in a position naively to try it out as an 'underground' assessment tool. My experience of the techniques I describe comes from working with the horoscopes of colleagues who have come to me as personal friends, and from friends who come to me as an astrologer, seeking help with personal problems that affect their work and relationships, a career decision, or for vocational guidance. The more my understanding of astrology develops, the more concerned I become about the privacy of the horoscope information. We live in an age when people are becoming acutely aware of the need for data privacy, and no data are more personal than the cosmic data of the birth chart.

Collecting the facts

Chart rectification

To set up a horoscope, the astrologer needs the date, time and place of the birth of the person. When a time cannot be given certain rules are followed in the hope of establishing a valid chart. The viability of such a chart is tested against important life events which should correlate with planetary positions at many levels. As the birth day is known, it is possible to establish a chart for the date of conception. The conception chart is another test and should mirror important reference points in the birth chart. If we are considering the use of astrology as an everyday tool for assessment, it is important to have the time of birth, as the technique of chart rectification demands the time of an experienced astrologer and consequently outprices itself.

Astronomical facts

Once the date, time, and place of birth are established, the astrologer calculates the chart, using the time of a true day which is four minutes shorter than the 24-hour day. This sidereal time and planetary positions are obtained from standard tables (the Ephemeris) based on Greenwich. Corrections are then made for time zone, longitude and latitude. One spin-off from the National Aeronautics and Space Administration (NASA) project is that very reliable computer-calculated tables of planetary positions up to the year 2000 are now published in a form that meets the need of the astrological market.

The planets move around the sun in the same plane and are observed through the same belt of sky (the ecliptic), which encircles the earth and crosses the Equator at the spring equinox. This intersection establishes the beginning of the tropical zodiac at 0° ♈ (nought degrees Aries). The ecliptic is then divided into 12 portions of 30 degrees, which are named with the 12 signs of the zodiac (see Fig. 8.1). Since the ancients first gave names to the star constellations, the earth's axis has shifted and the zodiacal zones along the ecliptic are no longer exactly in line with the constellations after which they were named.

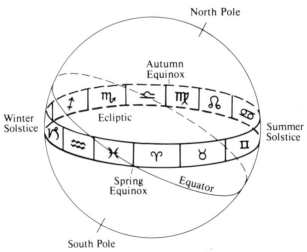

Figure 8.1   Planetary positions

The signs

Most people are now familiar with the 12 signs of the zodiac and the characteristics of these signs (Fig. 8.2). Linda Goodman[3] has written so well on the subject that I shall do no more than classify these under the elements of Fire (assertive), Earth (practical), Air (communicative), and Water (sensitive). Aries, Leo, and Sagittarius are Fire signs; Taurus, Virgo, and Capricorn are Earth signs; Gemini, Aquarius, and Libra are Air signs; Cancer, Scorpio, and Pisces are water signs.

Date	Sign	Symbol	Polarity	Element	Mode
March 21–April 20	Aries	♈	+	Fire	Cardinal
April 21–May 21	Taurus	♉	–	Earth	Fixed
May 22–June 21	Gemini	♊	+	Air	Mutable
June 22–July 23	Cancer	♋	–	Water	Cardinal
July 24–August 23	Leo	♌	+	Fire	Fixed
August 24–September 23	Virgo	♍	–	Earth	Mutable
September 24–October 23	Libra	♎	+	Air	Cardinal
October 24–November 22	Scorpio	♏	–	Water	Fixed
November 23–December 22	Sagittarius	♐	+	Fire	Mutable
December 23–January 20	Capricorn	♑	–	Earth	Cardinal
January 21–February 18	Aquarius	♒	+	Air	Fixed
February 19–March 20	Pisces	♓	–	Water	Mutable

SUN	☉	JUPITER	♃	
MOON	☽	SATURN	♄	
MERCURY	☿	URANUS	♅	
VENUS	♀	NEPTUNE	♆	
MARS	♂	PLUTO	♇	

Figure 8.2   The signs of the zodiac

Although the Sun sign continues to symbolize the nature of the very core of our being, Sun sign astrology must be left behind and the zodiac signs must now be considered as energies which also manifest themselves through the sign and house placement of planets.

The Ascendant

At the moment of sunrise, the sun is in the same position of the zodiac as the constellation zone that is coming up over the eastern horizon. If we take the example of a 'Sun sign Leo', someone born between 23 July and 23 August, this person will also have a Leo Ascendant if the birth is around the time of sunrise.

However, the daily rotation of the earth means that the zodiacal zone of Leo will continue to rise above the eastern horizon and will be replaced by the subsequent sign of Virgo. 'Sun Leo', born some three hours later with a rising sign of Virgo, is a very different person. 'Sun Leo' with a 'Leo Ascendant' is the one more likely to conform to the astrological stereotypes for this sign and may well be surprised by the apparent accuracy of newspaper and magazine astrology which is generally based on sunrise charts for each sign.

Once we recognize the importance of the signs on the Ascendant and Midheaven (the constellation zone directly overhead at the time of birth), it becomes apparent that knowledge of the 'Sun sign' alone is insufficient information on which to assess an individual. The rising sign colours the way others see us and how we present ourselves to the world. It is our 'persona', and can overshadow the Sun sign.

The angles

After establishing the Ascendant and the planetary positions for the birth time, the astrologer starts mapping the chart. The Ascendant and the Midheaven each mark an important axis. These axes locate four major points on the horoscope which are referred to as the 'angles'. When astrology is used for job assessment, the sign on the Midheaven is particularly important, as this marks the beginning of the tenth house, which relates to matters of career.

The houses

The chart is now divided into 12 houses. Tables of houses provide astronomical information which enables the astrologer to mark the house cusps around the outside edge of the chart. There is more than one system for establishing the positions of the house cusps, and the Placidean system has been used for the examples that illustrate this chapter. The differences between the various house systems and their respective merits are of little meaning to anyone who does not practise astrology; what is important within the context of this book is that the reader has a basic understanding of the areas of life experience that are related to each of the 12 houses. These are shown in Fig. 8.3. The meaning of the houses can be interpreted at many levels, and the key words given represent only the first layer of the onion.

The planets

Once the houses have been determined, the astrologer can mark the symbols for the planetary bodies (sun and moon now being described as planets) in their respective positions around the horoscope. The faster-moving planets move through signs fairly frequently and have a stronger effect at a personal level than the outer planets. An outer planet such as Neptune, with a cycle of 165 years, will remain in the same sign for many years. As an outer planet moves slowly through a particular sign its energy will certainly manifest collectively for a whole generation group.

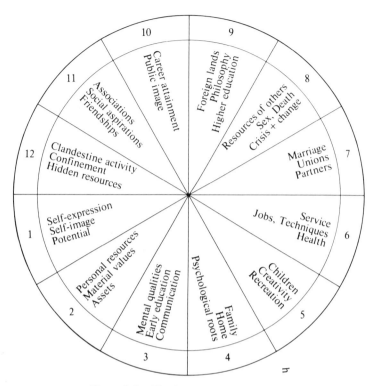

Figure 8.3   The houses of the horoscope

Figure 8.4 illustrates how the signs on the house cusps are different for the Leo born around sunrise and for the Leo born some three hours later the same day. The planets fall into different houses, and the moon, which is moving about one degree every two hours, has in fact changed sign from Virgo to Libra.

The aspects

When the planets have been placed within the chart the astrologer checks the angular relationships (the aspects) between them and marks these on the chart using different coloured broken and unbroken lines as a key to the relative strength of the aspects and whether the energies symbolized work with difficulty or with ease. The horoscope is now ready for interpretation, and begins to look somewhat like a printed circuit (Fig. 8.5). The more I work in a world of technology, the more I question whether astrology is some form of cosmic microcode and that the horoscope behaves like a 'cosmic chip'.

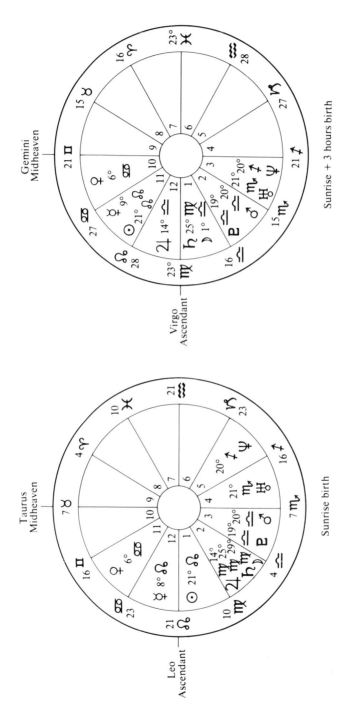

Figure 8.4 Sun Leo subjects

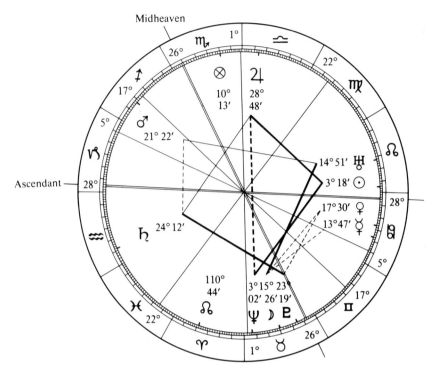

Figure 8.5   Horoscope of a psychologist

Interpreting the facts

Unique information

The astrologer now has the following information on which to base an interpretation of the horoscope:

(a) The planetary positions in signs and houses
(b) The aspects formed between planets
(c) The signs on the house cusps

In later examples I use two additional astronomical reference points which frequently indicate important contacts between charts: these are the positions of the moon's node (☊) and the part of Fortune (⊗).

Astrological tradition

The astrologer now draws from a great well of tradition dating back thousands of years, which covers:

(a) Planetary hierarchy
(b) Planetary rulership of signs and houses

(c) Main aspect patterns

(d) Positive and negative (spontaneous and passive) signs

(e) The elements of Fire, Earth, Air, and Water (assertive, practical, communicative, emotional)

(f) Cardinal, fixed, and mutable signs (initiating, consolidating and adapting)

Each planet symbolizes a life-principle or energy. A way of gaining a greater understanding of these principles is to study myths, legends, and fairy stories across many cultures. The circle containing a dot, which represents the Sun in a horoscope, symbolizes a source of life and vitality, a person's Will to Be, which will manifest itself according to the nature of the sign of the zodiac and the house position within the chart.

The three outer planets, Uranus, Neptune and Pluto, were discovered only in recent times and have been integrated into modern astrology. As knowledge of each planet's discovery entered the group consciousness, the world subsequently faced some major change. These planets have acted as harbingers of social and technical changes that inevitably affect all our lives. The powerful energies these planets symbolize did not manifest themselves in a tribal or feudal society. The astrologer therefore has to move with the times and with an understanding of the cultural and social background of the individual whose horoscope is being interpreted. The drama of life and the archetypal roles remain the same, but the scenery and the costumes change. The astrological symbols that suggest that a man will become a great warrior, who will have many fearless encounters on the battlefield against opposing tribes, are equally valid symbols when they are found in the chart of a female political leader of this century.

Figure 8.6 is a very elementary fusion of key words which will lead to a fuller understanding of the meaning of the planetary energies and the nature of the signs of the zodiac for the horoscope shown in Fig. 8.5. This information has then to be considered with regard to the energy patterns of the planetary aspects.

Judgement of the chart

The key words used in the examples represent a very elementary entry into the meaning of the astrological information. Words cannot replace symbols. A symbol is a means of contact with a vast storehouse of information which includes the collective unconscious, the personal unconscious, social and cultural heritage, family background, and recent personal experience. We only need to consider a symbol such as the cross or the American flag to recognize the energy, attitudes, and behaviour that the respective symbols have evoked at different points in history. Ask a group of colleagues or friends what a particular symbol means to them, and you will be surprised at the diversity of replies.

If we are endeavouring to treat astrology as an objective phenomenon, we have to ask how far it depends upon the consciousness of the astrologer who

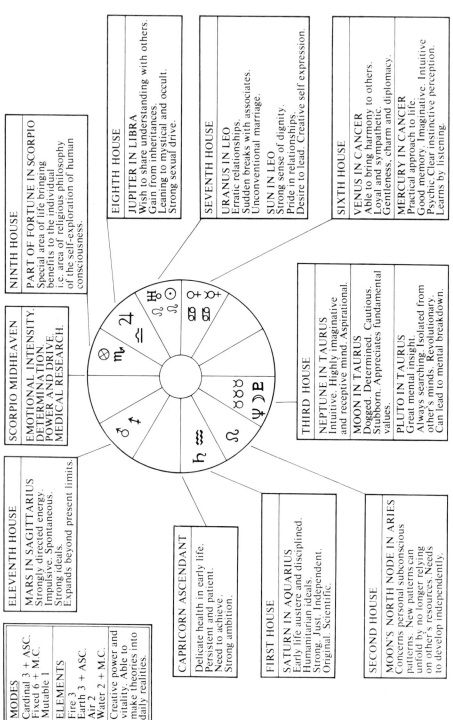

NINTH HOUSE

PART OF FORTUNE IN SCORPIO
Special area of life bringing benefits to the individual i.e. area of religious philosophy of the self-exploration of human consciousness.

EIGHTH HOUSE

JUPITER IN LIBRA
Wish to share understanding with others.
Gain from inheritances.
Leaning to mystical and occult.
Strong sexual drive.

SEVENTH HOUSE

URANUS IN LEO
Erratic relationships.
Sudden breaks with associates.
Unconventional marriage.

SUN IN LEO
Strong sense of dignity.
Pride in relationships.
Desire to lead. Creative self expression.

SIXTH HOUSE

VENUS IN CANCER
Able to bring harmony to others.
Loyal and sympathetic.
Gentleness, charm and diplomacy.

MERCURY IN CANCER
Practical approach to life.
Good memory. Imaginative. Intuitive
Psychic. Clear instinctive perception.
Learns by listening.

SCORPIO MIDHEAVEN

EMOTIONAL INTENSITY.
DETERMINATION.
POWER AND DRIVE.
MEDICAL RESEARCH.

ELEVENTH HOUSE

MARS IN SAGITTARIUS
Strongly directed energy.
Impulsive. Spontaneous.
Strong ideals.
Expands beyond present limits.

MODES
Cardinal 3 + ASC.
Fixed 6 + M.C.
Mutable 1

ELEMENTS
Fire 3
Earth 3 + ASC.
Air 2
Water 2 + M.C.

Creative power and vitality. Able to make theories into daily realities.

THIRD HOUSE

NEPTUNE IN TAURUS
Intuitive. Highly imaginative and receptive mind. Aspirational.

MOON IN TAURUS
Dogged. Determined. Cautious.
Stubborn. Appreciates fundamental values.

PLUTO IN TAURUS
Great mental insight.
Always searching. Isolated from other's minds. Revolutionary.
Can lead to mental breakdown.

CAPRICORN ASCENDANT

Delicate health in early life.
Persistent and patient.
Need to achieve.
Strong ambition.

FIRST HOUSE

SATURN IN AQUARIUS
Early life austere and disciplined.
Humanitarian ideals.
Strong. Just. Independent.
Original. Scientific.

SECOND HOUSE

MOON'S NORTH NODE IN ARIES
Concerns personal subconscious patterns. New patterns can unfold by no longer relying on other's resources. Needs to develop independently.

Figure 8.6   Information to be drawn from horoscope in Fig. 8.5

views the world with this symbolic language of astrology. The chart being judged is the map, and not the territory. It could just as well be the chart for the time a chicken is hatched, a spacecraft is launched, or a human being is born. A computer could easily synthesize the relevant bits of information from a vast data base and produce a judgement. But can a computer in fact produce a judgement? Let us look at the interpretation that a computer might give us when it searches for a meaning for Saturn in the first house:

(a) Inferiority complex, self-repressed nature
(b) Serious, industrious, and reliable
(c) Caution and introspection, which can bring success
(d) Early life austere and disciplined
(e) The birth was difficult for the mother

What the computer is not able to do is judge whether the individual is still spending his life trying to overcome a lack of self-confidence or whether, through an act of personal will, he has worked with determination to make a success of his life.

I have chosen this particular example of Saturn in the first house, especially when it is very close to the Ascendant, as it is frequently found in this position in the horoscopes of people who achieve more than most. If you are looking for a managing director, this could be a sure sign that you have a good candidate. However, you are probably already aware of this because his record supports your judgement.

What the horoscope cannot tell us about our subject is the IQ rating, the sex, and cultural background, which may have acted as additional constraining factors, or whether the subject was thrown into an environment that spurred him on to success. It is at this point that the astrologer uses intuition. The chart has been studied and enters the subconscious, where it picks up the rules and structures of astrology acquired by time-consuming study of the tradition. The details are then synthesized by the brain in much the same way as they are synthesized by the computer. However, the astrologer is now able to leave the mind free to sense the entirety of the chart, the pattern, and the potential within it. Feedback is now dependent upon the unique situation of the astrologer, the consciousness of the astrologer, and the astrologer's act of judgement, which requires perception and active imagination. Intuition is used to interpret what cannot be measured by technique alone.

Intuition

Intuition refuses to be pinned down and placed under the microscope so that we can examine how it functions. Personal striving and a desire to prove that it works only seems to interrupt the intuitive flow. When you stop trying to understand it, it trusts you and begins to work more and more effectively. The more you relax and allow it space in which to function, the more powerful it becomes. Examining intuition is like trying to capture the expression of a child for a photograph during the few moments when the light is right. As soon as the child becomes aware that it is the focus of attention, the whole energy of the situation changes; the child becomes camera-shy or shows off. The more you try to capture the moment, the more elusive it becomes. Such is intuition.

Intuition has traditionally been regarded as a feminine characteristic. It has probably been ascribed to the feminine because it cannot be attributed to a logical thought process which our society regards as 'masculine'. The more you surrender to the masculine principles of focus, objectivity, the need to measure and evaluate, quantify and organize, the more it will elude you. I am not suggesting there is any female prerogative. Instead, I believe it has something to do with a polarity other than masculine and feminine, a polarity of lateral and linear thinking. Intuition allows for a perception of realities not known to consciousness; it brings an understanding of symbolism and dreams—activities that involve the right hemisphere of the brain.

The study of symbols most certainly opens and strengthens the intuitive faculty, which leads me to the idea that the assessment tool may not be the horoscope at all. Its apparent efficacy as a means of judgement may be because the study of the symbols continually flexes the intuitive faculty of the astrologer like a cosmic exercise machine, developing it like a powerful muscle, and that the intuitive astrologer is simply using the horoscope as a focus for intuition. However, to suggest that the average person in a counselling, consultative, or management situation might study astrology for at least five years simply as a means of developing his intuitive faculty may seem a tall order. Let us consider instead what astrology can offer in practical terms as a method of assessment.

Astrology as a method of assessment

Astrologers are generally consulted on personal issues such as getting married, becoming divorced, conceiving a child, working in a foreign country, moving house.

At a professional level, astrology can be of interest in the following areas:

(a) Vocational guidance
(b) Recruitment and selection
(c) Team building
(d) Managing crisis and change

Vocational guidance

I believe this is a field where astrology can be of considerable value, as it raises no question marks about professional ethics if the astrologer works face to face with the individual, discussing the chart in a positive and constructive way. The client should then depart from the consultation with an understanding of his potential strengths, a recognition of the constraints he may need to overcome, and a feeling for the time-frame in which changes can occur if he chooses to take the opportunities offered. A major astrological work on vocational guidance[4] details assessment rules. The assessment focuses on the condition of the sixth house, which covers job, occupation, skills, and techniques as well as health (physical constitution being a closely related factor), and the tenth house, which is far broader as it covers career, vocation, profession, and public image. The sixth house of the horoscope of a young fashion designer may indicate that she has considerable flair and skill in her chosen craft. The tenth house and the Midheaven will give the clues as to whether she will extend this talent and become a household name with a great fashion empire behind her.

When all the specific vocational information has been sifted, the astrologer must still consider the chart as a whole and relate the symbolism in a very real way to the life circumstances of the individual.

My own experience of classic vocational guidance was disappointing, because it cut off many pathways where I failed to meet the academic requirements that were placed at the gateways to these routes. No one suggested that there might be a back door, or that I could exploit my abilities in a less orthodox way which could be equally fulfilling. I have been fortunate enough to work in organizations where there have been career opportunities beyond the imagination of the vocational guidance 'expert'; opportunities that could not be classified in a neat little package at the end of a flowchart. The vocational guidance consultant can perhaps be forgiven if the techniques he used did not give him much margin for lateral thinking. Astrology encourages lateral thinking, which should in theory increase the probability of determining vocational opportunities. This of course depends on the breadth of awareness of the astrologer, and we return once again to the question of the extent to which the interpretation depends upon the unique perception and judgement of the astrologer.

It is through astrology that I have since gained a better understanding of how I am motivated and in what type of environment I work best. Saturn in my third house is an indicator of a break in the educational process. Information such as this would be valuable to an interviewer who wants to test out an explanation for an educational gap. Saturn is symbolically limiting and constraining, and its third house position should have made me aware that any efforts to catch up as a mature student and get my 'piece of paper' validating academic achievement would require a considerable effort. Instead, I gained extensive experience and numerous skills, working primarily for two very large organizations. Big corporations and multinationals are symbolized by Jupiter because of the size and expansive quality of this planet. Jupiter is the ruler of my Sun sign, Sagittarius the centaur. This takes us into the world of mythology and to the centaur Chiron, who was the teacher to whom the heroes of the Grecian stories were taken as pupils. So Jupiter also symbolizes teaching, the very vocation I spurned when my school suggested it as the only career for a girl with the expectation of a good university degree. I have now come full circle and enjoy my work as an educator in a world of advanced technology. My moon is in Aquarius, a sign often found in the charts of people who work in the electronics industry, telecommunications, and the airline world.

If astrological vocational guidance had been available earlier in my life, would things have been any different? This raises the question of Free Will and Destiny. I believe that there are energies within us that flow forcefully in the manner and direction symbolized in the horoscope and that these must be reckoned with. At the same time, each one of us has freedom consciously to direct these powers at will once we understand them. For this reason, I strongly recommend astrology as a tool for vocational guidance and should like to see it being used from childhood to help each one of us to capitalize on our personal assets as well as to understand and control the drain made on our resources by the more difficult aspects symbolized within the horoscope.

Recruitment and selection

If we all had knowledge and understanding of our own horoscopes, we would apply only for jobs for which we recognized that we were entirely suited. The first few selection sifts would become unnecessary, and the interviewer could be left with a short-list of very suitable applicants for the job. Group compatibility might then become a major criterion for selection.

The use of Sun sign astrology for recruitment and selection is not recommended. Fragments of astrological information, like cards drawn from a shuffled pack, can be very deceptive. This is a time to stress the importance of holistic astrology: the whole person is greater than the sum of his chart.

Almost as a contradiction to this, I will describe the limited research I carried out on the charts of a sales group. They were working some years ago in a marketplace in which they could become successful. At that time success brought rewards in financial terms as well as fairly rapid promotions. What astrological significator shows sales success, and do we want this astrological factor to be part of the recruitment criteria?

Using only charts for which there was a known birth time, I placed the information from the horoscope on to the simple grid shown in Fig. 8.7. Eight out of the 12 have their Moon in an Earth sign. Half of this small sample have Moon in Virgo, which is described as 'reserved in expression, fussy about detail, industrious'. Is this our ideal marketing representative? As they are all men who would normally allow their energies to manifest strongly through the Sun sign and Ascendant rather than their moon sign, an indicator of emotional nature, we should look first to the sun sign, the Ascendant, and the Midheaven which is a strong indicator of career direction.

Figure 8.7 shows that there is a predominance of Leo in the Ascendant, Midheaven, and Sun sign columns. The nature of Leo was very suited to the sales role in the environment I described. Leo is ambitious, fearless, proud, assertive, and loves the limelight. A sales plan that motivates with rewards that also put Leo in the centre of the stage as 'Salesman of the Month' or even 'Salesman of the Year' keeps Leo very motivated. The rot may set in when you promote the person with Leo energy to a staff job which requires work behind the scenes. It is at this point that many people face a crisis of identity and have to start using other energies, perhaps developing a Virgo Moon.

Sales persons	Part of fortune	Moon's node	Rising sign	Midheaven	Sun	Moon	Mercury	Venus	Mars	Jupiter	Saturn	Uranus	Neptune	Pluto
	⊗	☊	ASC.	M.C.	☉	☽	☿	♀	♂	♃	♄	♅	♆	♇
1	4 ♑	8 ♏	2 ♌	6 ♈	10 ♉	12 ♎	13 ♈	7 ♈	21 ♑	28 ♓	23 ♈	17 ♉	21 ♍	2 ♌
2	20 ♑	1 ♈	15 ♌	29 ♈	3 ♌	8 ♑	20 ♌	5 ♋	21 ♎	6 ♓	17 ♍	7 ♋	15 ♎	17 ♌
3	19 ♓	13 ♏	29 ♌	16 ♉	16 ♒	6 ♍	6 ♒	29 ♐	4 ♐	8 ♓	14 ♈	14 ♉	22 ♍	0 ♌
4	15 ♓	19 ♌	27 ♌	15 ♉	1 ♊	20 ♑	2 ♊	14 ♋	27 ♓	22 ♋	14 ♊	4 ♊	29 ♍	5 ♌
5	12 ♓	11 ♐	24 ♎	2 ♌	25 ♌	13 ♑	22 ♍	15 ♋	4 ♐	18 ♑	4 ♈	13 ♉	17 ♍	29 ♋
6	12 ♒	16 ♌	12 ♒	14 ♐	7 ♌	22 ♋	19 ♌	16 ♍	15 ♉	6 ♌	22 ♊	8 ♊	29 ♍	7 ♌
7	21 ♋	16 ♍	14 ♌	22 ♈	24 ♑	2 ♑	9 ♒	21 ♒	2 ♉	12 ♊	22 ♉	26 ♉	29 ♍	5 ♌
8	16 ♎	11 ♊	13 ♌	25 ♈	8 ♋	6 ♉	3 ♌	3 ♋	28 ♋	9 ♉	12 ♉	25 ♉	23 ♍	2 ♌
9	21 ♓	11 ♏	13 ♌	25 ♈	17 ♓	25 ♎	2 ♈	3 ♒	23 ♐	15 ♓	17 ♈	15 ♉	22 ♍	29 ♋
10	24 ♎	18 ♊	4 ♍	26 ♉	8 ♌	27 ♍	25 ♍	21 ♍	10 ♌	20 ♎	29 ♋	20 ♊	6 ♎	11 ♌
11	15 ♈	2 ♉	25 ♍	23 ♊	26 ♐	17 ♋	29 ♐	27 ♏	16 ♑	7 ♑	6 ♍	28 ♊	14 ♎	16 ♌
12	21 ♋	32 ♍	29 ♋	1 ♈	17 ♍	9 ♍	13 ♎	29 ♌	25 ♍	19 ♋	12 ♊	5 ♊	29 ♍	6 ♌

Figure 8.7 Analysis of horoscopes of a marketing group

In this example you can see that the normal selection process quite successfully found 10 people who matched one possible astrological criterion. The Sun sign alone could not have revealed this, and an amateur astrologer using the simple technique illustrated instead of taking a holistic approach might have turned down the last two people, who did not fit the norm but were equally successful.

Astrology is being used for job selection, usually as an ancillary tool provided by astrologers who trust the integrity of the interviewer. This is usually in private companies who do not feel as exposed as large corporations to accusations of discrimination or invasion of personal data privacy, unless it is for a purpose of immediate social importance such as the selection of guardians of the law (policemen, magistrates, judges). I feel strongly that the information in the horoscope should not be revealed to a third party without the consent of the owner of the birth data, and I become extremely concerned when I see the 'sorcerer's apprentice' at work using a snippet of information and ignoring the holistic approach. This can be anything from a statement that top sales personnel are Leo to magazine articles that state categorically that Sagittarius and Pisces cannot have a good relationship. This subject of compatibility leads into the field of the dynamics of interpersonal relationships, where astrology can be used very valuably.

Team building

There is a growing interest in building balanced teams who can work in harmony, yet still have sufficient tension to maintain motivation, creativity, and productivity. Astrology can be of particular value as a method of examining interpersonal relationships. The technique, known as synastry, can be used with individuals, groups, and organizations. The astrologer takes each planetary position and notes what close aspects it makes to planetary positions in another chart. We are back to energy patterns running across two or more charts, and again the skill required is the ability to interpret the symbols in a way that has meaning for the individuals concerned.

As an example of how this technique can be used, I will quote the case of a bright young manager. He was given responsibility for a branch office with a group of salesmen that can only be described as 'a management challenge'. One of the salesmen confided to me his difficulties in relating to the new manager. Their relationship degenerated to a point when it monopolized every conversation I had with the salesman, whom I will now refer to as Bob. The lack of communication between Bob and his manager created a gulf into which Bob projected everything negative about anything. At that stage, all I could offer was support as a listener, and it is only now, when I study the synastry between the charts, that I notice that the position of Mars in the manager's chart is right opposite Bob's Saturn. The Mars–Saturn contact has a bad reputation; these two energies are likely to engage in bitter conflict and fight to the finish. If the battle is unresolved, there is a war of attrition that kills off any communication. At the same time, I notice that Bob's Sun is in the same position of the zodiac as the manager's Moon. This is the classic compatibility combination. If these two men had understood the energy patterns, they could have consciously chosen to take the Sun/Moon route to establish an acceptable working relationship instead of remaining locked in the Mars/Saturn stranglehold.

Because the technique of synastry puts a focus on the archetypal energy symbolized in the horoscope, it defuses a lot of the emotion that arises when the problems of a difficult relationship have to be brought out into the open. The isolation of the energy in the form of a symbol allows it to be handled and consciously redirected.

In addition to using synastry to aid one-to-one relationships within a group, it can also be used for balancing the assets of a group. A chart such as that shown in Fig. 8.7 could reveal a innovative and go-ahead group which never gets down to serious planning because there is a lack of Earth in the group. An astrologer can suggest the astrological components needed to complement the group, but this is as tricky as blending a palette of hundreds of colours in an endeavour to get a perfect shade match.

Managing crisis and change

Finally, I want to look at how astrology can enable us to understand and support other people as well as ourselves at a moment of crisis or change.

Astrologers frequently refer to the planets as though they have personalities of their own and are working as an autonomous force within the individual, colluding in a way that forces the ego to take note of the inner energies that are pushing in their own direction. At times of crisis, it often feels as though these energies are taking control, particularly when they are accompanied by very real external events.

There are several cycles of change that an astrologer immediately recognizes when a horoscope is prepared. Some of these show up when the astrologer uses a technique known as chart progression. Other changes are synchronous with planetary transits to the birth chart. One occurs at about the age of 28 or 29, when the transit of Saturn is again occupying the same zodiacal position as it did in the birth chart. The Saturn return brings about a consolidation of life's circumstances, which may not be uncomfortable if your life is in order, but can be very difficult if you have been running away from certain responsibilities or necessary decisions. Many people race into marriage, have their first child, race out of marriage, or establish their career at this stage.

Another major transit occurs at about the age of 42, when the planet Uranus completes half of its cycle. It appears in the heavens opposite the place it occupied in the birth chart. Change at this time often comes like a lightning flash, although the circumstances causing the change may have been brewing for some time. Many people suddenly find themselves made redundant or with some type of career or life direction crisis. We must not forget that crisis is also opportunity. Many women who have brought up a family suddenly decide around this time to change their lives radically, and often leave a long established marriage to travel the world or to start a career of their own.

Crisis and change do occur at other times. Many people hit one at about 35; others may seem quite random. However, they never occur without some very strong astrological correlation. The value of astrology in these circumstances is that, through the symbolism of the chart, it is possible to understand the meaning of the crisis and to recognize the opportunity the change will bring. The astrologer can identify a time-frame in which the effects of the crisis will continue to be felt and can suggest ways in which the individual could best direct his or her energy to contain the situation and grow through it.

An increasing number of counsellors and therapists are now studying astrology or using it to support their major discipline. Astrology is a symbolic language which seems to be more readily accepted in this field than others. Psychotherapists are also used to examining taboos, and for many astrology is still a taboo subject. The necessary regard for privacy, trust of personal information, and avoidance of judgement also encourages the co-operation of the astrologer. As the horoscope is such a wonderful map and guide to the psyche, astrology works extremely well with psychotherapeutic techniques such as active imaging and guided imagery. It is in the field of personal development and inner growth that I see the use of astrology developing most rapidly in the future. This is where I believe this powerful tool will be used with the integrity it deserves.

References

1. Jung, C. G., 'Synchronicity: An acausal connecting principle', in *The Structure and Dynamics of the Psyche* (*Collected Works of C. G. Jung*, vol. 8), 1952.
2. Ostrander, S. and Schroeder, L., *Astrological Birth Control*, Prentice-Hall, Englewood Cliffs, NJ, 1972.
3. Goodman, L., *Linda Goodman's Sun Signs*, Pan Books, London, 1972.
4. Luntz, C., *Vocational Guidance by Astrology*, Llewellyn Publications, Saint Paul, Minnesota, 1962.

Recommended further reading

Arroya, S., *Astrology, Psychology and the Four Elements*, CRCS Publications, California, 1975.

Dean, G., *Recent Advances in Natal Astrology*, The Astrological Association, Bromley, Kent, 1977.

Davison, R., *Synastry: Understanding Human Relations through Astrology*, ASI Publishers, New York, 1977.

Gauquelin, M., *The Cosmic Clocks*, Peter Owen, London, 1969.

Greene, L., *Relating: An Astrological Guide to Living with Others on a Small Planet*, Coventure, London, 1977.

Oken, A., *The Horoscope, The Road, and its Travelers*, Bantam, New York, 1974.

Progoff, I., *The Symbolic and the Real*, Coventure, London, 1977.

Watson, L., 'Man and the cosmos', *Supernature*, Hodder & Stoughton, London, 1973.

West, J. A. and Toonder, J. G., *The Case for Astrology*, MacDonald, London, 1970.

9. Astrology: Fact or fiction?

DAVID K. B. NIAS

From the ancient Greeks to the isolated Mayans, most of the major cultures in the world have incorporated a belief in astrology. Even today, many people believe that the exact moment of birth has some mysterious association with personal development and success in life: current surveys in the Western world indicate that nearly half the adult population believe that there is some truth in astrology. This widespread belief extends even to university students. For example, in a survey at the University of Pretoria, C. Plug[1] found that 49 per cent of the students answered 'yes' to the question, 'Do you think that there is something in astrology?'

Rightly or wrongly, belief in astrology has affected the lives of people throughout history. The ancient Egyptians preferred to recruit Scorpios as their warriors on the basis of a belief that people born under this sign possess an 'intense, passionate, and vindictive' character. Hitler commissioned astrologers during the war to make predictions that would have propaganda value. Even today, we hear of people choosing a marriage partner on the basis of 'astrological compatibility' and of people being selected for a career on the basis of an astrologer's recommendation.

Are people right in assuming that astrology contains an element of truth? According to the astrologers themselves, they are, but according to most scientists whose opinion has been sought, they are not. An astronomer, G. O. Abell,[2] went so far as to claim that 'I doubt if I could find a single physical scientist who holds any belief whatsoever in astrology.'

Leaving aside the possibility that astrologers themselves may be biased, we must ask whether their testimony throws any light on the matter. They are, after all, the experts, and some of them have spent a lifetime studying the astrological literature. But sad to say, their beliefs appear to be based on nothing more substantial than folklore and intuition. It might even be possible to make a case for the value of intuition, were it not for one insurmountable problem: that contradictory beliefs are held by the leading practitioners of astrology. Traditional astrology is not quite the same as modern astrology, and Western astrologers work from a set of principles different from those of

Eastern astrologers. Moreover, even within countries there are many differences of opinion depending upon which particular school of astrology one ascribes to.

If the experts themselves disagree over the details of astrology, how do we decide who, if anyone, is right? A parallel situation exists in psychology with the theory of psychoanalysis. Freud's original theory differs slightly from Jung's, which in turn is different from Adler's, and so on. There has been much debate as to whose authority should be trusted, but a lasting solution to the dilemma has been found only by conducting experiments to settle the issue. In other words, answers have been sought by letting facts decide between the points of disagreement. As it happens, the experiments have so far indicated that none of the psychoanalysts is correct and that conventional psychological principles are sufficient to provide explanations, anyway. Following this solution to the controversy over psychoanalysis, there is no reason why the validity of astrology should not be put to the test in a similar way.

It would thus be argued that the opinion of astrologers is worth considering only if they can support their claims with factual evidence. To assert that the position of the planets at birth is associated with certain character traits is hardly convincing if no one has taken the trouble to check whether such an association really exists. Fortunately, a few intrepid pioneers have attempted to provide such evidence, and their claims deserve to be taken seriously. Similarly, the opinion of scientists is worth considering only if they have familiarized themselves with the available evidence. Unfortunately, very few scientists have more than a fleeting acquaintance with the research, and it is only the opinion of these few that can be taken seriously. But it is possible to do better than merely to seek the opinion of recognized experts: we can actually examine the research studies, as well. Unlike research in most scientific subjects, astrological studies are straightforward and non-technical enough to be open to evaluation by the layman.

Astronomy and astrology

It should at this point be emphasized that there are two major aspects to the work of an astrologer. The first is the construction of a map of the heavens at the time of a person's birth, and the second, an interpretation of what this means for the individual. The first stage involves the relatively exact science of astronomy, and so agreement between astrologers is near perfect. The second stage, which essentially represents the astrologers' contribution, involves what may be nothing more than subjective belief, and many discrepancies are apparent between different astrologers. Most astrologers tend to overlook the distinction between the accuracy with which they construct the birth chart and the accuracy with which they interpret it; they often give the impression of being confident of their ability at both stages of the process.

This all-important distinction was clearly made by Claudius Ptolemy of Alexandria, who wrote the first major survey of astrological doctrine. To quote from the *Tetrabiblos*: 'We shall now give an account of the second and less self-sufficient method in a properly philosophical way, so that one whose aim is the truth might never compare its perceptions with the sureness of the first, unvarying science.' What a pity that modern astrologers have not paid more heed to these words of their eminent predecessor.

Evidence for astrology

How strong is the evidence for astrology? There has been no shortage of research into the subject. In a classic and monumental survey, Geoffrey Dean and colleagues[3] searched over 1000 books and hundreds of journals for evidence in favour of astrology. Precious few studies could be found that provided positive evidence. In the vast majority of studies the evidence was negative or at best ambiguous. Even for the basic Sun signs, better known as signs of the zodiac, Dean and his team were unable to find any clear demonstration of their validity. Prompted by this, and by the continuing insistence of astrologers that there must be a link between Sun signs and personality, G. Dean and A. Mather[4] offered a prize of £500 to anyone who could substantiate a claim for any such link. As Dean and Mather pointed out, 'if signs are valid then they can be shown to be valid. Opinions or beliefs will not do; we want facts.' To date, no one has made a serious claim for the prize; this perhaps speaks for itself. The conclusion reached by Dean and his team still holds, namely: 'the evidence . . . suggests that the success and acceptability of Sun-sign astrology owes nothing to astrology and everything to gullibility'.

Other reviewers have reached a similar conclusion. In our own survey,[5] we were able to find fault with almost all the studies purporting to provide evidence in favour of traditional astrology. A negative conclusion applied even to the popular notion of the full moon affecting the mentally unbalanced. Two independent reviews of research concerned with the effect of the moon on murder, suicide, and mental health also failed to reveal any positive findings that stood up to scientific scrutiny,[6, 7] To quote from the former: 'It is concluded that lunar phase is not related to human behavior and that the few positive findings are examples of . . . error.'

A negative conclusion also applies to the assumed link between time of birth and occupational success, at least as far as signs of the zodiac are concerned. A basic claim in astrological textbooks is that Sun signs help in revealing character and in predicting occupational success. A few researchers have, indeed, reported finding such a connection. But a consistent and repeatable trend has not been found for any one occupation or Sun sign. Dean and his team demonstrated that agreement between researchers is apparent only for studies involving an overlapping sample of eminent doctors, scientists, sportsmen, or whatever. For studies where truly independent samples have been selected, the degree of agreement becomes negligible. This indicates that the few positive findings were due to chance—otherwise they would have survived replication. An apt conclusion of the current status of Sun sign astrology was expressed by R. B. Culver[8] with an adaptation of the words of Sir Winston Churchill: 'Never before in human history has so much been based on so little by so many.'

The first astrological study to appear in a psychology journal was concerned with occupational success. P. Farnsworth[9] put a well-known astrological maxim to the test. According to most schools of astrology, people born under Libra tend to be artistic because this sign is ruled by Venus, the planet of the arts and of beauty. But after examining the birth dates of 7233 musicians and artists, Farnsworth found that Libra was no more common than any other sign. Similarly, in a recent survey of 10 313 university graduates, G. Tyson[10] found that their Sun signs were not related to the subjects they had studied. This negative evidence, of which many similar examples could be given, provides a strong counter-argument to the claims of astrologers on the validity of Sun signs.

Season of birth

Having disposed of Sun signs, we must now ask the more general question: namely, whether season of birth is related to human characteristics. One of the most impressive sources of evidence concerns confirmation of the popular notion that geniuses tend to be born in winter. In 1938 Ellsworth Huntington[11] published the results of his monumental survey on the season of birth. The most striking finding to emerge from his survey was that 'famous' people, as listed in the *Encyclopedia Britannica*, tended to be born in mid-winter. Defining eminence in terms of the amount written about them in the *Dictionary of American Biography*, Huntington also demonstrated that the mid-winter peak became more and more marked for the more eminent.

Using the latest edition of *Encyclopedia Britannica*, A. Kaulins[12] decided to check the finding concerning famous people. In order to eliminate the possibility of selection bias, he plotted the birth dates of all the people listed—a total of over 11 000. Figure 9.1 shows that Huntington's finding of a February peak was clearly supported by this enlarged sample. Also plotted is the average temperature in New York City over the year, which closely parallels the birth graph and shows that eminent people tend to be born at what is typically the coldest time of year in the Northern Hemisphere. In contrast, for the general population there is little variation in the birth rate during the year. In the UK there is a slight peak during the spring, while in the USA there is a slight peak in the autumn.

Since Kaulins's result is based on such a large sample, there can be little doubt as to its authenticity. Replication is hardly appropriate, since the sample already represents something approximating the total population. But what can be done is to sub-divide the sample in terms of level of eminence, as Huntington had done for famous Americans, in order to confirm that the result becomes even clearer for the more famous. Apart from this, one can begin to seek explanations for the result.

According to Dryden, 'Great wits are sure to madness near allied, and thin

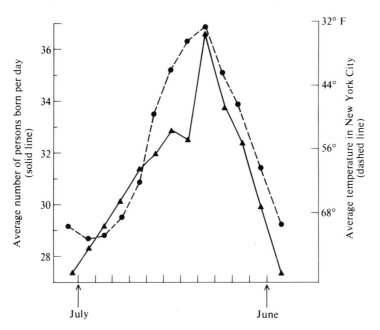

Figure 9.1   Persons listed in the **Encyclopedia Britannica** *tend to be born during the month of February, which for most of them represents the coldest time of year (based on Kaulins[12])*

partitions do their bounds divide.' It is perhaps more than coincidence that surveys of the birth dates of psychotic patients also reveal a February peak. In noting the similarity of results obtained in surveys among the mentally ill, E. Hare[13] was sufficiently impressed to write that a mid-winter birth peak provides 'the first clear association between the incidence of schizophrenia and a simple, objectively definable factor in the environment'.

Why geniuses and the insane should tend to be born in mid-winter, or under the signs of Capricorn, Aquarius, and Pisces, if you are astrologically inclined, is at the moment inexplicable. It is presented here as evidence that it is not unreasonable to suggest that a person's character and ability are related to the time of year that he is born. What is unreasonable is confidently to assert reasons, whether astrological or otherwise, as to *why* this should be so. The finding can at the moment only be presented as a fact that is 'stranger than fiction'.

Sources of error

Before turning to evidence that supports astrology more directly, it may help to illustrate how positive evidence must be subjected to thorough examination before being even tentatively accepted. A good example is provided by the effects of a subject's knowledge on the outcome of a research project. In most psychological research, it is recognized that subjects should be naive in case they are influenced by knowing what it is that the experimenter is trying to measure. So, too, in astrological research, it is possible that individuals who know about astrology will be influenced by this knowledge in their responses to, say, a questionnaire. Our own research has been directed towards investigating this possibility.

The starting point was a study by J. Mayo, O. White and H. Eysenck,[14] which had apparently demonstrated the truth of the astrological maxim that outgoing or extraverted personality types tend to be born under the odd-numbered signs of the zodiac (such as Aries) while reserved or introverted types tend to be born under the even-numbered signs (such as Taurus). The results obtained from a sample of 2324 people who completed a personality questionnaire are shown in Fig. 9.2. The obtained zig-zag pattern clearly shows that the astrological hypothesis was supported, and consequently it was proclaimed by some astrologers that science had vindicated their discipline.

The possibility remained, however, that some of the people, in completing the questionnaire, had been influenced by knowing the type of personality that they were meant to possess according to astrology. For example, an Aries person might have been more likely to endorse the question, 'Are you bold and energetic?' if he happened to know that Ariens are meant to possess these very characteristics.

It was obvious that the research needed to be extended to include people who were naive about astrological matters. Our next step was to repeat the research on a sample of children for whom it could be assumed that knowledge of astrology was much less than for adults. Data from a sample of 1160 schoolchildren aged 11 to 17 provided results that were clear-cut; there was no indication at all of the zig-zag pattern obtained with adults. With this sample of presumably naive subjects the astrological hypothesis was not supported.

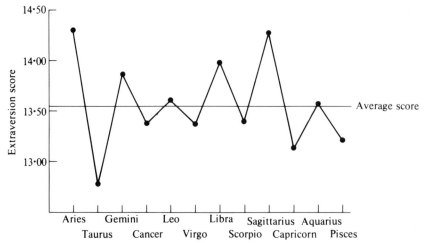

Figure 9.2 *The extraversion scores of people tend to follow the predicted astrological zig-zag pattern (based on Mayo et al.[14])*

The next step was to find out if a group of naive adults would also fail to support astrology.

If people are asked if they know anything about astrology, some will answer 'no' merely because of natural modesty. Therefore, in order accurately to classify people as knowledgeable or not, it is safer to make use of an objective procedure. We did this for a sample of 122 adults recruited from evening classes and from the Salvation Army. An objective test was designed, consisting of an astrological profile listing the personality traits representing each of the 12 signs. These 12 sets of traits were presented in random order, and the subjects' task was to indicate which one represented their own sign. Many of the subjects protested that they had no idea which was which, but they were instructed to guess, being told that they should have at least a vague idea on the basis of incidental knowledge gained from friends, relatives, newspapers, and magazines. Of the sample of 122, no less than 46 correctly identified, at the first time of asking, the set of traits associated with their own sign. This group was labelled 'knowledgeable'.

Before this test the subjects had been assessed for personality by asking them to select from the 12 sets of traits the one that best described their own personality. At this stage they were not aware that the research was concerned with astrology. The critical analysis was to see if there was any tendency for this self-assessment of personality to correspond with the astrologically predicted one. It did, but only for the 'knowledgeable' group. For the group of people who were unable to identify the set of traits associated with their own sign, there was no tendency for personality to correspond with astrological prediction. This part of the result was thus consistent with that obtained with children.

A similar study on adults has been independently conducted in Germany by K. Pawlik and L. Buse.[15] A translation of the personality questionnaire used in the original study by Mayo and colleagues was completed by 799 subjects. Another questionnaire was designed to assess each person's degree of belief in, and hence familiarity with, astrology. Consistent with our own finding, it was only the group of people who believed in astrology that displayed the astrological zig-zag effect.

On the basis of the results from these studies, it appears that people who possess some knowledge of astrology will be influenced, to at least some extent, in their replies to a questionnaire; an assessment of their own personality will tend to match that which corresponds with their own sign. Since such an outcome is apparent among people possessing some knowledge of astrology but not among those specially selected as naive, it will be necessary in future to adopt the practice of deliberately selecting naive subjects for astrological research.

Planetary influences

One area of astrology in which it can be safely assumed that most people are ignorant concerns the position of the planets at the exact moment of birth.

And it is only from research on this topic that a convincing case can be made for astrology. The research concerns the work of Michel Gauquelin and his wife Françoise. Gauquelin is acknowledged as the world's leading researcher into astrology. Over the past 30 years he has conducted many pioneering studies of such potential importance that his efforts have been compared with those of Charles Darwin. To start with, his studies on basic astrology provided uniformly negative results. Two examples will suffice.

According to traditional astrology, Aries is meant to signify a predisposition to adventure, accidents, struggle, fights, and rivalry. In order to test this theory, Gauquelin[16] looked to see if Aries was over-represented among men to whom this description seemed particularly appropriate. He chose a group of 1995 French generals, but after examining their birth dates found that Aries was no more common than any other sign.

Similarly, according to tradition, Mars is meant to be prominent in the birth charts of people associated with violence, blood, and crime. Murderers on file in the Paris Courthouse were chosen as the test group for this theory. A group of 623 of the most notorious murderers was selected, but nothing was found in their birth charts to indicate the horror of their crimes or even their own destiny—which in most cases was death under the guillotine. Mars was not even over-represented in the eighth astrological house, which is meant to represent death.

These are only two examples of the negative outcome studies that Gauquelin has conducted. Having made such a convincing case against the basic tenets of astrology, he might have abandoned this line of research. But among all the negative results, there was one positive result that kept appearing. This concerned the tendency for one of the major planets to be just above the Ascendant or rising point (the eastern horizon) or just past the Midheaven (the point directly overhead) in the birth charts of famous people.

Just as the sun appears to rise in the east and to set in the west, so too do each of the planets appear to rise and set as the earth spins on its axis. Gauquelin divided each planet's 360-degree cycle into 12 sectors of 30 degrees each. These sectors correspond roughly to the astrological houses, and it was noted that for famous people the planets were over-represented in the first and fourth sectors starting from the eastern horizon. Distinguished physicians, for example, tended to have Mars or Saturn in one of these two sectors at the time of their birth. For actors and soldiers it was Jupiter, for scientists it was Saturn, while for writers it was the Moon. In contrast, for the general population, birth times were spread evenly over all 12 sectors with around $8\frac{1}{3}$ per cent of births occurring in each.

Surprised by his finding, Gauquelin has repeated the analysis many times on various groups. Almost every time the result has been confirmed. It is only for successful people and for extreme personality types that the pattern emerges, and it is only for particular occupations or personality types that particular planets are implicated. One of the best researched findings has been the tendency for Mars to be in one of the key sectors at the birth times of famous sportsmen. This has become something of a test case.

In his first study involving 2088 renowned European sportsmen, Gauquelin[17] found that 21.5 per cent were born when Mars was just past the Ascendant or the Midheaven, as shown in Fig. 9.3. This compares with an expected value of one-sixth, or $16\frac{2}{3}$ per cent, and because of the large sample size is highly significant statistically. Figure 9.3 also shows that a control group of 717 ordinary sportsmen were born at times that corresponded closely to the general population. This link between Mars and sporting prowess was made the subject of a special inquiry by the Committee for the Scientific Investigation of Claims of the Paranormal. This American organization has the express aim 'not to reject such claims on *a priori* grounds, antecedent to inquiry, but rather to examine them objectively and carefully'.

Evaluation

The Committee, led by P. Kurtz and colleagues,[18] decided to repeat Gauquelin's research on a sample of American sportsmen. But an obstacle to their endeavour arose in the form of the US Privacy Act, which prohibits state departments from providing personal information without the consent of the individuals concerned. Because some of the states interpreted this to include birth times, data were obtained for only a fraction of the sample originally selected. For what it is worth, 19.5 per cent of 128 sportsmen were born with Mars in one of the two key sectors. Because of the inconclusive nature of this

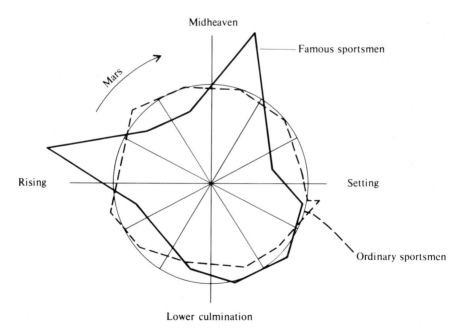

Figure 9.3   Sportsmen tend to be born when Mars is just past the Ascendant or Midheaven only if they are famous. The circle represents the expected distribution of births for the general population (based on Gauquelin[17])

result, the sample was extended. Analysis of a new total of 408 cases revealed that only 13.5 per cent were born 'under' Mars.

The Gauquelins[19] discounted this result on the ground that the sample had not met an important criterion, namely that the sportsmen be truly successful. In an attempt to obtain a sufficient number of cases, the Committee had included sportsmen who could not be regarded as of national, let alone international, class. Moreover, because the selection had been made from publications that list thousands of sportsmen, such as *Who's Who in Basketball*, even coaches had been included! The Gauquelins pointed out that their own research had repeatedly demonstrated that the Mars effect applies only to the highly successful. For example, no Mars effect was apparent for 599 players in the Italian Football League who had not achieved international status.

The Gauquelins attempted to demonstrate further the principle that, the higher the standard of achievement, the stronger the Mars effect. They subdivided the US sample in terms of achievement. They selected 88 cases as representing the highest levels of sporting achievement. For the 88 superior sportsmen, the Mars effect was significantly stronger than for the remaining 320 lesser sportsmen. In particular, the Mars effect was apparent for no less than 35 per cent of 20 Olympic champions. On the basis of this more detailed analysis, the Gauquelins concluded that the Mars effect was supported by the US data.

The response from the Committee was that in their opinion the sample represented a similar level of achievement to that of Gauquelin's original sample of 2088 European sportsmen. Since the aim of their research was to replicate the original study, they considered their approach to have been vindicated. Further, with regard to the Gauquelins' subdivision in terms of achievement, they noted that six Olympic champions including Muhammad Ali had been inadvertently omitted. (These cases had in fact been left out because the Gauquelins kept strictly to the *World Almanac and Book of Facts*, which does not list team or boxing medallists.) If these extra cases are included, the Mars effect applies to a slightly less impressive 31 per cent. The Committee also selected its own list of 53 eminent sportsmen from the ranks of basketball, football, and boxing, and found that a Mars effect applied to only 15 per cent of them. Thus, on balance, the Committee stood by its conclusion that their study had failed to support the claim of a Mars effect.

What can we conclude from the above? At first glance, the US data indicate that the Mars effect is of a 'now you see it, now you don't' nature. This is not untypical of research findings in psychology, where it is comparatively rare for an original result to be clearly replicated at each attempt. All too often a clear-cut result fails to survive even a first replication attempt. But this has not really happened in the case of the Mars effect. The Gauquelins' division of the sample in terms of achievement, by covering all the sports, seems more convincing than the Committee's selection in terms of just three sports. This is especially so since the Gauquelins had earlier noticed that European basketball players were an exception to other sportsmen in not revealing a Mars effect. Looked at in this light, the Committee's finding provides partial confirmation rather than disconfirmation. Moreover, there have been other replication attempts, and these too need to be taken into account before reaching a verdict.

The Comité Para in Belgium, an organization parallel to the US Committee, conducted its own replication study on 535 European sportsmen. Unfortunately, the organization has been strangely silent about its findings, and full details of the investigation have never been published. But it appears that the Mars effect was supported with 22 per cent of cases falling into this category. The Gauquelins have also conducted their own replication studies. The latest included a new sample of 432 European sportsmen who were selected only if 'their reputations had gone over the frontiers of their own country and ... their performances had been remarkable in international competitions'. This group revealed a Mars effect of 24 per cent.

Conclusion

By considering all the evidence, and taking into account the vagaries of research, a tentative conclusion is possible. This conclusion seems to be that outstanding sportsmen really do show a slight tendency to be born when the planet Mars is in one of two particular positions in the sky. Why this might be so is of course totally inexplicable. But it may be noted that the two positions—the rising point and the Midheaven—are close to what have long been considered the most important of the 12 astrological houses. Moreover, Mars has been traditionally associated with war and, symbolically, sport might not seem too far removed from this!

To this evidence on sportsmen must be added the findings relating to personality and to other occupations and planets. In total, the evidence provides a very strong case in favour of a central aspect of astrology—namely, the position of the planets at birth. Full details of Gauquelin's work have been published in a series of documents, and so the research is open to independent checking and evaluation. No one has yet succeeded in seriously faulting his research in terms of design or analysis.

In considering possible applications of Gauquelin's findings, a word of warning is in order. The effects are very small, having required very large samples of people to detect. For example, a Mars effect of 22 per cent as opposed to the expected birth frequency of $16\frac{2}{3}$ per cent means that only an extra five or so out of every 100 sportsmen are 'astrologically typical' in being born under Mars. The remaining 78 per cent are the exceptions, having succeeded as sportsmen in spite of having been born at the 'wrong time'. This, of course, is in line with the astrological maxim that 'the stars incline, but do not compel'. The often overlooked implication of this principle is that knowledge of a person's birth time has only slight predictive value. Sport would have been the poorer if 78 out of every 100 champions had decided, on astrological grounds, to pursue a different career! It is perhaps for this reason that most astrologers have been loath to incorporate Gauquelin's findings into their beliefs. In general, they prefer to work only from the more dogmatic assertions of traditional astrology.

This chapter has not painted a very rosy picture of astrology in general. But for the scientist, if there is any truth at all in astrology, then it is of the most profound importance. All that is known about the universe precludes the possibility that the position of the planets at the time of birth can in any way be associated with personal development and destiny. However, if Gauquelin's findings continue to survive investigation and checking, then science will somehow have to acknowledge them as facts in need of explanation. It will be interesting to see what happens.

References

1. Plug, C., 'A psychological study of superstitious behaviour', Ph.D thesis, University of South Africa, 1973.
2. Abell, G. O., 'One astronomer's views', *The Humanist*, January 1976.
3. Dean, G. A., Mather, A. C. M. and 52 others, 'Recent advances in natal astrology: a critical review, 1900–1976', Analogic, Perth, 1977 (distributed by Recent Advances, 36 Tweedy Road, Bromley, Kent; and in the USA by Para Research, Whistletop Mall, Rockport, Mass.).
4. Dean, G. and Mather, A., Letter to the *Astrological Journal*, vol. 21, p. 89, 1979.
5. Eysenck, H. J. and Nias, D. K. B., *Astrology: science or superstition?*, Maurice Temple Smith, London, 1982.
6. Campbell, D. E. and Beets, J. L., 'Lunacy and the moon', *Psychological Bulletin*, vol. 85, pp. 1123–9, 1978.
7. Cooke, D. J. and Coles, E. M., 'The concept of lunacy: A review', *Psychological Reports*, vol. 42, pp. 891–7, 1978.
8. Culver, R. B., *Sun sign sunset: A scientific look at the claims of Sun sign astrology*, Pachart, Arizona, 1979.
9. Farnworth, P. R., 'Aesthetic behavior and astrology', *Character and Personality*, vol. 6, pp. 335–40, 1937.
10. Tyson, G. A., 'Occupation and astrology or season of birth: A myth?' *Journal of Social Psychology*, vol. 110, pp. 73–8, 1980.
11. Huntington, E., *Season of Birth: Its Relation to Human Abilities*, John Wiley, New York, 1938.
12. Kaulins, A., 'Cycles in the birth of eminent humans', *Cycles*, vol. 30, pp. 9–15, 1979.
13. Hare, E. H., 'Season of birth in schizophrenia and neurosis', *American Journal of Psychiatry*, vol. 132, pp. 1168–71, 1975.
14. Mayo, J., White, O. and Eysenck, H. J., 'An empirical study of the relation between astrological factors and personality', *Journal of Social Psychology*, vol. 105, pp. 229–36, 1977.
15. Pawlik, K. and Buse, L., 'Selbst-Attribuierung als differentiellpsychologische Moderatorvariable', *Zeitschrift für Sozialpsychologie*, vol. 10, pp. 54–69, 1979.
16. Gauquelin, M., *The Cosmic Clocks: From Astrology to a Modern Science*, Paladin, St Albans, 1973.
17. Gauquelin, M., *Cosmic Influences on Human Behavior* (2nd edn), ASI, New York, 1978.
18. Kurtz, P., Zelen, M. and Abell, G., 'Results of the US test of the "Mars effect" are negative', *The Skeptical Inquirer*, vol. 4, pp. 19–26, 1979.
19. Gauquelin, M. and Gauquelin, F., 'Star US sportsmen display the Mars effect', *The Skeptical Inquirer*, vol. 4, pp. 31–43, 1979.

Acknowledgement

The help of Professor H. J. Eysenck during the preparation of this chapter is gratefully acknowledged. The material reported is presented in greater detail in H. J. Eysenck and D. K. B. Nias, *Astrology: Science or Superstition?*

10. Palmistry: A critical review

ROWAN BAYNE

Palmistry claims to measure personality, abilities, and state of health from characteristics of the hands. It also claims to measure events, past and future; but I am not concerned here with predicting the future except in the sense that descriptions of personal qualities are also predictions. Although palmistry is a very speculative area of study, I do not think any possible measure of personality should be easily rejected, not even those that it is generous to call 'less conventional'. This view is based on three general points: the high value of even small improvements in the accuracy of personality assessment, the crude nature of present techniques and theories, and the relatively low cost of research into personality.

The first part of this paper touches on possible applications of research into three aspects of palmistry: beliefs consistent with palmistry, or parts of it, the theory of personality underlying palmistry, and palmistry as a medical test. Any value that these three aspects may have does not depend on the validity of palmistry as a psychological measure. The main section describes what palmists do, discusses a rationale for relating personal qualities to hand characteristics, and reviews several studies of whether they actually are related or not.

Beliefs

Any belief we have about people's appearance or behaviour can influence, perhaps unfairly, our perceptions of their personalities. For example, we may believe that a firm handshake is a sign of honesty, that long fingers are artistic, that small hands are more capable of detailed work than large ones. As far as I know, very little research has been done on such beliefs, though Jahoda[1] reported that 36 per cent of a first-year psychology class agreed that people with long fingers are likely to be artistic. Jahoda did not try to find out whether this belief was justified. It might be worthwhile doing this. Suppose, for example, that a selector of management trainees believed that 'artistic' people (a) have long fingers and (b) make poor managers, and used length of fingers as a basis for selection. The *consequences* of his or her belief would be real, whether the belief itself was true or not. Alternatively, it may be that, other things being equal, long fingers do indicate some kind of artistic ability.

Palmistry's theory of personality

Psychology's personality theories are at present varied and promising rather than definitive. Thus, one reason for studying palmistry's theory is that it may be the theory that psychologists are working towards, or, more likely, that it may suggest the beginnings of such a theory or some parts of it: what to measure rather than how to measure it. I will suggest a few perspectives, using a passage from a chirologist* as a starting point. Spier[2] wrote:

> I base my approach on the assumption that man is born with definite dispositions which in normal cases determine his intellectual and spiritual development at least in part.... Most people, however, because of wrong education and haunting impressions from childhood which have produced disturbances and inhibitions, are unable to adopt that attitude to life which is in accord with their actual dispositions. ... Apart from ascertaining the character, the talents, the unconscious influences, the effects of the milieu, it is [the task of the chirologist] to find out how and by what a person is prevented from leading a life according to his own natural dispositions, how and why a person is again and again compelled to go through certain experiences which bind and limit him. ...

Spier's is a complex theory, only partly constitutional. He sees most people as having a 'basic' personality which somehow survives 'underneath' or 'behind' those acquired aspects of personality that are inconsistent with it. Among psychology's theories, Maslow's is the most similar. For example, he described man's 'inner nature' as 'easily overcome by habit, cultural pressure, and wrong attitudes towards it', and added that 'Even though denied, it persists underground forever pressing for actualization.'[3]

Thus, socialization is seen by both Maslow and Spier as either enhancing or, more often, impeding development of a 'basic' personality or self. Many psychologists—for example, Carl Rogers, Eric Berne, R. D. Laing—agree on a concept of inauthenticity or 'defensiveness', that generally people are alienated from aspects of themselves, and that healing can take place. They disagree on the nature of the self from which people are seen as alienated.[4] For palmists, certainly for Spier, the basic personality is something definite, predisposing one person, for example, towards gardening and being sociable (among other qualities), and another towards music and solitude.

I think that this concept of particular behaviours being 'constitutionally right' for each person is both appealing and disturbing. In the very act of providing an apparently real basis for self-definition, it also sets limits. However, palmistry is not completely deterministic: it claims that personality *change* registers in the hands—not only change away from the disturbances mentioned by Spier, but improvements on one's 'basic' personality.

---

* Chirology is an alternative term for palmistry. It is less emotive but also tends, unfortunately, to be confused with chiropody.

One problem with the concept of predisposition, i.e., Spier's 'definite dispositions' which exist at the moment of conception, is that it provides an easy 'escape' when predictions fail. 'Ah,' the palmist can say, 'it's there, you *are* like that. but it's still potential, you just haven't developed it yet.' Some projective testers take a similar, 'safe' position, as do astrologers. This does not mean, though, that the concept is untestable, and therefore outside science. For example, a group of people could be assembled all of whom behave, say, unassertively. Some of these people would, according to a palmist or other 'expert' in personality assessment, be 'really' assertive underneath; others not. After finding out if the two groups differed in ways consistent with self-actualization theory, all the people would then be trained to behave assertively and their success measured. If the groups of 'really' assertive and 'really' unassertive people differed in their experiences of the training and/or their degree of success, both the concept of predisposition and the method of measuring the particular predisposition would be supported.

Another complication in considering palmistry's theory of personality is that not all palmists agree. For example, an interesting alternative approach is that most people *do* know themselves, that their predispositions *do* affect behaviour directly. On this view, the notion of 'latent talents' is too romantic: if someone is talented, it shows (given a 'reasonable' environment) and has at least been dabbled in. The palmist's role, it is argued, is to describe the person's qualities, to encourage him or her to make more effort, and to listen. For my purposes here, it is enough to show that one palmist's theory of personality is compatible with some major theories in psychology and that it provides what may be a vital concept: that of 'definite dispositions', which are submerged or brought out, rather than changed, by socialization.

Palmistry as a medical test

There is some apparently good evidence linking hand characteristics to disease, especially congenital disease.[5,6] It is suggested that abnormalities in hand shape, in the dermatoglyphics (the fine lines at the level of fingerprints), in fingers, and in crease-lines indicate increased *probabilities* of finding more important abnormalities elsewhere in the body. Part of the rationale is that the lines form in the womb at a time when the foetus is most vulnerable to viruses and other harmful conditions. Scheimann,[6] who is both a GP and a palmist, claims that young adults who die after violent exercise are 'often' found to have congenital heart abnormalities, and that these could have been diagnosed early from the hands, and their deaths perhaps prevented. Numerous other illnesses, including two of particular interest to personnel managers—stress and alcoholism—are said to be indicated by hand characteristics before they are apparent in other ways.

I have not the appropriate specialist knowledge to discuss this aspect of palmistry further. In any case, it is largely separate from palmistry as a personality test; i.e., it could be true and valuable and the personality predictions not. Moreover, although medical evidence appears straightforward, there are bound to be problems. To illustrate this, the following points, among others, need to be considered by medical researchers when evaluating any form of diagnosis or treatment.

GPs, witch-doctors, palmists—indeed, anyone who diagnoses and treats illness—are likely to appear more effective than they really are, partly because most illnesses are minor and self-limiting: patients recover regardless of diagnosis and treatment and sometimes in spite of them. Yet we tend to attribute the cure to the person we consulted. Another factor is that expert attention, or attention seen as expert by the patient, reduces uncertainty and anxiety regardless of the particular expertise, diagnosis, or treatment, and particularly for psychosomatic illnesses. In addition, many patients with chronic illnesses occasionally feel better, as part of the 'natural course' of their illness. The general point is that personal testimony of the value of a particular method of diagnosis is not good evidence for the accuracy of that method.

To summarize so far: the consequences of beliefs in aspects of palmistry— attributing artistic ability to a person with long fingers, for example—are real, regardless of whether the beliefs are true or not; I have discussed the possible value of palmistry in developing an integrated theory of personality, with special reference to the concept of predisposition; and touched on the subject of palmistry as a medical test. However, it would be wrong to argue, by extension from the medical evidence—which includes, in Down's Syndrome, a striking correlation between distinctive characteristics of both personality and hands—claims for palmistry as a personality test: these need to be tested directly.

What palmists do

The hand characteristics that palmists study include the way the hands are held; the fingers, nails, and thumbs; the backs of the hands; qualities such as texture, flexibility, consistency, shape, and size; and, of course, the lines. Two types of line are distinguished: the dermatoglyphics and the so-called 'crease' lines. Generally, the characteristics used by palmists are relatively static and tangible. This is in comforting contrast to the elusive personal qualities that they may represent.

There are two, complementary, approaches to palmistry; the technical, or thinking, and the emotional, or feeling. The *technical* approach is to study someone's hands carefully and systematically for two or three hours (using prints for most of that time); while the *emotional* approach is to try and reach the same goal—a fairly full and accurate personality description—much more quickly and without conscious detailed analysis. My interest is mainly in the first of these, which is comparable to map-reading. An example of this approach is the claim that, other things being equal, a long little finger indicates greater 'managerial ability' than a short one. I will add quickly that the evidence for this claim is very slight, and a specific rationale non-existent, but also that it is a precise and testable hypothesis.

Palmistry's rationale

What ideas have been suggested as explaining the relationship, if there is one, between hand characteristics and personal qualities? We have the necessary conditions—enormous variation in (a) personality and (b) hands—but why should managerial ability be correlated with the length of a finger or vitality with the quality of a 'crease' line? There are several possibilities. The first is that both physique and personality are genetically based. For example, using Sheldon's term, ectomorphs are said to be both angular and fond of solitude as a result of their genes. However, no strong relationship of this kind has been found, and the basis of any link between physique and personality is not clear; it could for example be due to social expectations and stereotypes rather than to genes[7] (but cf. the earlier argument on testing the concept of predisposition).

In any case, the hands would, on this argument, be simply a convenient part of the body by which to judge overall physique and at best a general mechanism with no relevance, for example, to the lines, except perhaps to their overall quality. A valid classification of the kind proposed by Sheldon would be a major breakthrough for personality research, but only general support for palmistry. The endocrine glands are a similar general mechanism. According to Wolff, the major researcher on the hand,[8] everyone has a characteristic endocrine syndrome which affects the shape of their hands and fingers, and their temperaments.

A third and potentially more specific mechanism is suggested by the very large number of nerve endings in the hands compared with most other parts of the body. Some palmists suggest that the process is two-way. I have one piece of evidence, at the level of a case-study, which may provide a dramatic illustration of this mechanism. It consists of the handprints of a student who was unconscious for 36 hours after a bicycle accident: the 'head'-line in her right hand looks as if it has been 'snapped'. (She appears to be functioning well now, and is a GP.) I have not seen a similar head-line in hundreds of hands, nor the hands of other people who have been unconscious for long periods. St Hill[9] described the related case of a painter who had fallen from a scaffold and suffered severe concussion. He was unconscious for two weeks. Apparently every line on his hands vanished during the first week; then as he recovered consciousness they gradually reappeared.

Although this fading phenomenon is said to be rare,[10] the general claim that lines are affected by impulses from the brain could be tested on the hands of dead people: presumably, if it is true, their lines should vanish. Watson[5] states this as a fact. He writes:

> Throughout life, even in deep sleep, the many fine muscles of the face are in states of variable tension produced by constant stimulation from the brain. The total effect of these waves of activity is to produce a pattern which gives each face its unique features. . . . It is likely that a similar supply goes out from the brain to all parts of the body and constantly reinforces form and function. The exact pattern of the palm print, like that of the heartbeat or the life field, seems to depend on the maintenance of these signals, because the lines in the hand begin to break down when the impulses cease, at the moment of death.

Hutchinson[10] also argues that the lines are not 'crease'-lines, or not only crease-lines, because they do not correspond to the way our hands fold: there are lines where there are no folds and folds without lines. But this may be just a characteristic of skin.

Finally in this section I will mention two specific possibilities. The mound at the base of the thumb may be affected by the arteries underneath it and may in turn affect the so-called 'life' or vitality line, which sweeps in a semi-circle round it.[10] On this view, looking at the life-line is rather like taking a pulse but provides a more permanent record. Second, Wolff[8, 11] made several specific suggestions based mainly on the rationale that lines record hand movements. For example, versatile and subtle hand movements, especially movements of the fingers, are seen as associated with particular lines and with power of self-expression. One such line—the 'girdle of Venus', to use the palmists' name—is seen by Wolff as being due to separate movement of the third and fourth fingers in hands which are especially mobile. The suggested link between mobility of hands and power of self-expression or any other characteristic still needs to be explained, however. Wolff's view of the lines as crystallized gesture may complement the suggested direct two-way link between the brain and the hands.

Palmistry's rationale, then, consists of suggestions that it is easy to cite in the abstract: physique, endocrine glands, genes, impulses from the brain, involuntary expressive movements. They are areas for exploration rather than a good theory, but lend credence to the possibility that there is 'something there'. In any case, it is quite defensible to take the very pragmatic, atheoretical approach of most books on palmistry and to say, in effect, 'It works. How it works is a separate question.'

Palmistry as a measure of 'normal' personality

Most books on palmistry are catalogues. They are based on anecdotal evidence, which is very open to exaggeration and selective memory. Science rightly treats such evidence with scepticism. The essence of scientific method is to protect us against our fallible memories and perceptions so that anecdotes and assertions, even those based on thousands of years of study and made by persons of the highest integrity, are treated as hypotheses. Science requires that observations be replicable and *generally* true. Thus, my own head-line changed (in palmistry's terms, 'strengthened') as I worked for my final examinations. I have 'before' and 'after' prints to 'prove' it. But the scientific interest is more in head-lines generally, with such questions as: 'What proportion of students' head-lines change in their last year?' and 'Is there any relationship with other variables, e.g. a knowledge of palmistry or previous laziness?' As another example, Gettings[12] included 'before' and 'after' prints of an alcoholic who recovered after three years' psychotherapy. This is interesting, but again we need to know whether it is representative or a special case, a fluke.

My first investigations of palmistry were of personal experience and thus at the lowest, but still important, level of scientific evidence. I looked at my hands and those of people I knew. And, in what I saw then as a crucial test, I visited a mental hospital. The first patient's hands were, from palmistry's point of view, magnificent: exceptionally strong indications of depression and submissiveness, even to someone who knew little about palmistry. Ironically, this was the most striking case, though most of the other patients had hands that seemed fairly abnormal. I also visited a mental hospital for children, with similar results.

There have been some more systematic investigations of palmistry, four of which will be discussed in the rest of this section. First, in Wolff's study,[13] 69 subjects each put his or her hands through a hole in a thick curtain for about 15 minutes and did not speak. Handprints were taken and notes of shape, fingers, etc., made. Then Wolff wrote an interpretation. For example, one subject was described as, among other things, having 'overflowing vitality', 'a very marked emotionality ... strongly sexual and erotic ... excessive in everything', 'so restless that he likes a quick change of surroundings and adores travel and expeditions', 'a great lover of nature', 'very generous', 'original and revolutionary', 'a good orator and clever with his fingers'.

This seems to me a rich and individual personality description. Wolff also took some quite sophisticated precautions. Thus, she noted that 'as far as possible generalities were avoided, those qualities which distinguish one person from another being emphasised', and she also attempted to control what would now be called the 'social desirability' of the statements: were the relatively flattering ones accepted more readily than the unflattering? The next stage is to find out how true the descriptions are. Wolff's method of assessing accuracy was as follows: each subject was given a list of personality statements, half of which were taken at random from all 69 interpretations and half from his or her own interpretation, and asked to select 'any qualities which appear to be characteristic of your own personality. Choose about 50% of the items.'

Unfortunately, the data were analysed inappropriately: the significance values of chi-squared tests were based on numbers of observations rather than numbers of subjects. This is technically known as an 'inflated N', and tends to give spuriously high values, as it did in this study. From the data as presented, the only justified inference is that Wolff was judged right slightly more than half the time, which is not very impressive. However, Wolff also argues that there were two distinct types of subject: those who tended to agree with her (i.e., if she was correct, demonstrated self-awareness) and those who tended to contradict (i.e., those who were self-alienated). This interesting possibility needs to be checked with further research, which would try to identify those who demonstrated self-knowledge and those who demonstrated lack of self-knowledge, *before* analysing the results.

Wolff also tested her data in two other ways. First, subjects read through their descriptions and agreed or disagreed with each part of them. They agreed with almost three times as many as they disagreed with, but the 'Aunt Fanny' or Barnum phenomenon[14] obviously cannot be ruled out. The second was a little more satisfactory. A class of 11 female students were each given copies of the personality interpretations of all of them and asked to decide (a) which was her own interpretation and (b) which belonged to each of her fellow students: 6 students correctly chose their own; 3 students 'who had extremely similar personalities' chose each other's interpretations; and 1 of the 2 students who did not select her own was easily and correctly matched with her interpretation by the rest of the class.

Wolff recognized the major drawback of matching studies: if successful, they show that judgements can be made, but not the information used to make them, and it may be just on one possibly trivial detail, like physique. Thus, the description itself is not necessarily validated in this way. In this study the descriptions are not provided, and without them it is not possible to evaluate the analysis further; but usually a successful matching study is taken as indicating that further research is worthwhile.

In another study, Wolff[11] tackled the problem of a correct answer to the question, 'What is this person like?' as follows: 19 girls all aged about 11 were assessed by Wolff, and her descriptions locked away without anyone else seeing them. Descriptions of the children were collected from their teachers after a year and again after another four years. Thus, the teachers were used as 'experts'—which, as with self-report, begs the question of a 'correct' perception of personality, but is worth trying.

One of the teachers wrote up the results after the five years, commenting that 'By this time there was every reason for feeling that the children were well known'.[11] She gives Wolff's descriptions and summaries of the teachers' descriptions. For example, Wolff wrote:

> A strong child with good physical dynamism. A simple elementary personality, inclined to be materialistic with too little capacity for sublimation. Emotionally dull but a tendency to be impulsive. Gifts on the purely physical side—gardening or swimming.

The summary of the teachers' views was:

> A well-developed child with no intellectual or aesthetic interests and very indifferent home. Good physical ability—always friendly and pleasant. Quite content to be behind the rest of the class in most of the work and to muddle along uncertain of anything. A poor mentality.

The teacher who wrote up the descriptions commented: 'A perfect agreement'. However, there are problems: no mention of 'impulsiveness' in the teachers' assessment, for example, and what does 'too little capacity for sublimation' mean? The problems of what *terms* we should use to describe personality, and what they mean, is illustrated well. I think though that, over the 19 cases, Wolff's descriptions are generally clear, subtle, and individual. So it is particularly unfortunate that the teacher summarized her own and her colleagues' ratings, thus allowing the possibility of bias, and that the method of assessing accuracy was purely impressionistic. Also, Wolff saw the children, not just their hands; she may even have talked to them. Over all, the study, despite its strengths, is at best suggestive.

A much more recent study by Fox[15] is worth mentioning. He looked at the relationship between dermatoglyphics (in this case, fingerprints), extraversion–introversion, and neuroticism–stability. Dermatoglyphics are formed by the third or fourth month of life in the womb, like the 'crease-lines'; but unlike the crease-lines these elegant patterns do not change. As Fox pointed out, this gives them great potential as a measure of temperamental aspects of personality. He reported a relationship between rare categories of fingerprints and low neuroticism, but does not provide enough information about his methods to justify a firm judgement.

Some palmists infer personality characteristics from the dermatoglyphics of the hands, e.g., that composite loops on the thumbs indicate indecisiveness, and arches lack of trust, of oneself and others. Such claims seem like much of palmistry, to be examples of thinking at the level of very simple analogies; but, again, they are testable.

My own research

Wolff and palmists stress the holistic nature of their subject. They argue that all the hand characteristics need to be taken into account and balanced against each other before good assessments can be made. Each sign can contradict or give greater emphasis to another. For example, a 'girdle of Venus' is seen as more significant in square palms than in long ones. This is a dangerous aspect of holistic personality assessment, although, given the complexity of persons, it is probably also necessary. The danger is that if a particular prediction fails another hand characteristic can usually be found to explain it and make a new prediction, thus 'explaining' the failure.

My own research used an analytic approach, testing a hypothesis relating a single feature of the hands to personality. The particular hypothesis was concerned with the position of the line that runs from the lower part of the hand towards or to the base of the middle finger. Palmists call this the 'fate-line'. The position from which the fate-line 'begins' is often interpreted in terms of restriction by parents or relatives of a person's early life. Independence or lack of restriction is shown (it is claimed) by a hand in which the fate line and life line (which circles the large mount at the base of the thumb) are clearly separate and the fate line starts from near the base of the palm. Restriction is shown if the fate line is joined to the life line, or if the fate line starts nearer the middle of the palm than the wrist.

This choice of hypothesis has several virtues. First, as I said, a relationship is claimed that is not affected by other parts of the hand, or by the type of hand. Second, the hypothesis is extreme; if it is true, then much of palmistry is more likely to be true as well. Third, the interpretation is obscure. The problem here is that, if people know what their own fate-line is said to indicate, they may believe it *for this reason*. (As a precaution, I also asked subjects if they knew which the fate-line was.) Finally, the concept of 'early restriction' is used in some selection procedures. Crudely, the argument is that attainments should be considered against background, usually social class, type of school, etc. On this argument it is, for example, seen as more creditable to get to Oxford University from a village school than from Eton.

My subjects were 80 students, 15 members of a community centre, and 8 members of an evening class. They answered a questionnaire of five items on their early experience. A 'yes' answer to any *one* of the items was taken to indicate that the subject experienced his cr her early life as restricted. I also examined, without knowing the questionnaire responses, the preferred hand (the one used for writing) of each subject, and, by simple inspection, classified each subject as 'restricted', 'not restricted', or 'indefinite' (details of the criteria are available from the author).

No prediction was made for subjects classified as 'indefinite'. My hypothesis was that 'restricted' subjects would be more likely to give at least one 'yes' answer to the questionnaire than subjects classified as 'not restricted'. This prediction was confirmed (Table 10.1), particularly striking being student/non-student, and therefore age, differences: students tended to be 'not restricted' on both measures, the older non-students to be restricted on both. The results were also statistically significant for the student group analysed separately (Table 10.2).

Table 10.1 Responses to questions on 'early restriction' by subjects with and without clearly separated 'fate' and 'life' lines (all subjects)

	Lines joined or 'fate' line starting late	Lines clearly separated	Not classified
Yes to one or more items	20	7	17
No to all five items	7	16	36

Chi = 13.1 $P < 0.01$ $n = 103$

Table 10.2 Responses to questions on 'early restriction' by subjects with and without clearly separated 'fate' and 'life' lines (students only)

	Lines joined or 'fate' line starting late	Lines clearly separated	Not classified
Yes to one or more items	9	6	12
No to all five items	6	16	31

Excluding cases which were not classified, $P < 0.05$ (Fisher's exact probability); $n = 37$

The item, 'I feel that my early development was hampered and suppressed', was the most powerful, but each item was the distinguishing one for some cases. Some 'restricted' subjects were also interviewed. One said 'I found I thought what my parents would think before I thought what I would think'; another that 'My father is a very high-powered academic, and I felt overshadowed and stupid.'

The relationship between (perceived) early restriction and the position of a line was then in the direction predicted by palmists. There are four possible explanations of these results. The first two accept them at face value: (1) that the person's perception of his or her development, whether accurate or not, caused the position of the fate line; (2) predispositional, that people born with fate-lines in the restricted position have a tendency to view themselves as restricted, a kind of innate melancholy.

Assuming for the moment that one of these explanations is true, why was the relationship not a perfect one? One obvious reason is that restriction is vaguely defined and crudely measured. Another possibility is that subjects whom it was predicted would respond in the restricted direction and did not (of all subjects: 7 out of 23) were restricted too well, and did not realize it. Thus Cheiro[16] wrote: 'there is every likelihood of the owner following a parental profession or business and feeling that it is just and right to do so'. This is the same kind of *post hoc* explanation used in Wolff's distinction of two kinds of subject: those who agreed with her and those who disagreed. And, again, it is testable.

The other two interpretations of the results are critical of my methodology. The first is that I might well have realized that age and questionnaire responses would be correlated and therefore distorted my perception of the older group's fate-lines. Against this interpretation, the students' results—and the students were all about the same age—were significant in their own right, though less so than for the whole sample. The second interpretation in terms of method is based on the fact that I saw people and not just hands, and so it is possible that in some way I guessed their questionnaire responses often enough to make the results non-random. Again, for this to be true I would have had to distort my perception of the lines. Neither of these possibilities can be decisively ruled out; they can only be investigated in another experiment.

Table 10.3 Responses to questions on 'early restriction' by subjects with three positions of 'fate'- and 'life'-lines (students only)

	Lines joined	'Fate'-line starting late	Lines clearly separated	Not classified
Yes to one or more items	3	6	6	12
No to all five items	5	1	16	31

The relationships in Tables 10.1 and 10.2 were quite strong by the standards of personality research, but when I split the results for the two kinds of line interpreted as 'restricted' (a distinction made in the experiment itself) there was a very strong relationship for lines 'starting late' (Table 10.3). Strictly speaking, this was not a hypothesis, so no statistical test was carried out. But it also is not open to the usual objection, a very important one, that extensive reworking of data can lead to spurious 'positive' results just through chance. The distinction between the two kinds of 'restricted' lines was made in the experimental procedure itself. Nevertheless, the finding should be replicated.

Special strengths of palmistry and conclusions

If it does measure personality, palmistry has some special strengths First, it seems likely to be a very reliable test: trained raters should usually agree with each other. In addition, the palmists' assessment should not be influenced by the candidate's or client's boredom, enthusiasm, suspicion, tiredness, naïvety, etc., and faking should not be a problem. (I suspect though that, if it proves necessary, ways of faking will be found: perhaps plastic surgery, or a combination of mental exercises and drugs?) Further, the person whose hands are looked at is usually trusting: what is loosely called 'rapport' seems to develop quickly. Palmistry's acceptability to candidates for a job or for promotion may nevertheless be doubtful (even though interviewing is accepted!). A final strength is that palmistry is not very expensive: for a high-level managerial post, say, two or three hours of an expert's time.

The following aspects of palmistry seem to deserve further attention from psychologists and other scientists: beliefs in aspects of palmistry, palmistry's theory or theories of personality, and palmistry as a medical test. Palmistry's rationale in terms of genes, endocrine glands, movements, and impulses from the brain is easy to cite in the abstract but provides areas to investigate rather than explanations. The evidence on palmistry as a measure of personality is by no means conclusive, but I think is worth following up. In particular, *abilities* should be related to hand characteristics, as they provide clearer criteria than personality variables.

References

1. Jahoda, G., *The Psychology of Superstition*, Pelican, Harmondsworth, 1969.
2. Spier, J., *The Hands of Children*, Routledge & Kegan Paul, London, 1955.
3. Maslow, A. H., *Toward a Psychology of Being*, Van Nostrand, London, 1968.
4. Bayne, R., 'The meaning and measurement of self-disclosure', *British Journal of Guidance and Counselling*, vol. 5, pp. 159–66, 1977.
5. Watson, L., *Supernature*, Hodder & Stoughton, London, 1973.
6. Scheimann, E., *A Doctor's Guide to Better Health Through Palmistry*, Prentice-Hall, Englewood Cliffs, NJ, 1969.
7. Lindzey, G., 'Behaviour and morphological variation', in J. N. Spuhler (ed.), *Genetic Diversity and Human Behaviour*, Aldine, Chicago, 1967.
8. Wolff, C., *The Human Hand*, Methuen, London, 1942.
9. St Hill, K., *The Book of the Hand*, Rider, London, 1927.
10. Hutchinson, B., *What your hands reveal*, Spearman, London, 1967.
11. Wolff, C., *The Hand in Psychological Diagnosis*, Methuen, London, 1951.
12. Gettings, F., *The Book of the Hand*, Hamlyn, London, 1965.
13. Wolff, C., 'Character and mentality as related to hand markings', *British Journal of Medical Psychology*, vol. 18, pp. 364–82, 1941.
14. Hampson, S. E., Gilmour, R. and Harrison, P. L., 'Accuracy in self-perception: The "fallacy of personal validation"', *British Journal of Social and Clinical Psychology*, vol. 17, 231–5, 1978.
15. Fox, G., 'Does the finger point at you?' *New Behaviour*, 142–3, 24 July 1975.
16. Cheiro, *You and Your Hand*, Jarrolds, London, 1969 (originally published 1933).

Postscript

D. MACKENZIE DAVEY and MARJORIE HARRIS

This brief final chapter is deliberately headed 'Postscript' rather than 'Conclusions', as would be more usual. The reader may well have formed his own opinions already on some of the skills of judging people described here. If he has not, we do not feel we can do more than offer him some tentative pointers along the way. We do not want to patronize his intelligence, nor do we want to risk making platitudinous comments. That said, we will try to summarize and to offer him some final thoughts to guide him through the maze.

This has been a fascinating book to assemble, and we hope that the reader too has been intrigued by some of the approaches. As we noted in the Introduction, our choice of subject matter has been selective rather than comprehensive, and, when inviting authors to contribute on less conventional techniques, we have concentrated on those who have tested their theories and practice and have subjected their findings to research. Even so, some of the possibilities put forward may well seem somewhat unorthodox.

So where do we stand in the business of judging people? Any reader hoping to have found a new and speedy method of understanding and predicting behaviour must inevitably be disappointed. His only hope may lie in a point made by Eysenck in his Foreword, in which he says 'different people have differential powers to judge others, some being very good at it, others very bad'. Investigations of what is sometimes called intuitive judgement reveal a great deal of evidence that gifted judges do exist. These are people who can in a short time make remarkably accurate judgements of others. But one difficulty here is that most people appear to believe that they *are* one of these gifted judges. Regrettably, there seems to be no relationship between the *confidence* with which people make their diagnoses and the accuracy of their *judgement*.[1] Vernon and Parry reported[2] on a WREN (Women's Royal Naval Service) whose personal predictions were consistently better than those of the objective tests, which in turn were superior to those of most interviewers. (Her personal validity co-efficient was 0.55 compared with 0.39 for the objective measure.) At the other end of the scale, there are those who are consistently wrong. They too, of course, could be valuable: one could do just the opposite to what they advised! But there would appear to be no reason why, in the field of personnel selection, gifted judges should not be identified and used, backed by other carefully chosen techniques.

Little is known about the characteristics of the skilled intuitive judge and how he or she differs from less able associates. Investigations indicate that good judges are of above-average intelligence (but many highly intelligent people are poor judges: high intelligence is necessary but not sufficient). They also have had experience of meeting large numbers of people. Thus, in general, older people (because they have met more people) are rather better judges than younger. Even this generalization is distorted by the finding that we are better at judging those *like* ourselves than those *unlike* ourselves. Therefore men are better at judging men, women at judging women, the young at the young and the old at the old. (Most studies, incidentally, give little support to the value of 'women's intuition'.) Even if it is not feasible to find a 'genius' judge, great care should be taken in the selection of selectors.

In his chapter (Chapter 6) on the psychology of interpersonal perception, Cook has some harsh things to say about the way we judge each other, whether we are laymen or experts. 'Whenever a person's ability to say what someone thinks, or feels, or intends to do is put to a proper test, that person's performance barely exceeds chance level.' Sadly for the 'experts', including psychologists, findings show that they are no better than laymen at predicting what someone will do next. Cook is equally unhappy about the concept of intuition—'a faculty unrecognized by scientific psychology'. He notes a number of possible meanings of this concept and would not quarrel with 'intuition' if what is meant is a skill so thoroughly learned that one is not conscious of its operation. He concludes that the evidence is heavily against those who claim that judgements based on intuition are better than predictions made by conscious processes of inference based on information of proven value. Cook sticks closely to a basic making-inferences-from-cues-of-proven-validity model of human judgement, and his last sentence reads: 'At least if one sticks just to trying to guess what the other man is going to do next, one will know if one is right or not.' Such simplicity makes salutary reading when one encounters more pretentious theories advancing claims for authenticity!

For the foreseeable future, at least, it would seem that most people who are professionally concerned with judging others—those in personnel selection, for example—must rely largely on conventional established techniques. Even the interview, that most widely used of all selection tools, can be conducted differently and with different levels of success. If the interviewer is to be successful he must be selected and also trained. Bayne's chapter (Chapter 5) on the interview includes some points on a counselling skills approach to selection interviewing. This assumes that interviewers want to collect relevant inform-ation, attract good candidates, and, lastly, leave candidates who are not successful feeling that they have been treated fairly. In summary, he believes that interviewing as it is currently practised is a poor method of judging people. But other methods also have marked weaknesses, and there seem to be many possible ways of improving interviewing. For example, certain approaches to training can help, as can candidates' views of interviewers' strategies and their own. But Bayne sees basic counselling skills as lying at the heart of an integrated approach to interviewing and of the problem of determining its limits as a technique for judging people.

Mackenzie Davey (Chapter 3) also takes a somewhat jaundiced view of the interview on its own. 'How well does the average interviewer assess a candidate's intelligence? It is common experience that he or she does it badly, but with great confidence: a dangerous combination.' But he does hold that careful interviewing can provide valuable data, especially when it is carried out by trained interviewers. Bayne touches on what little research has been done on the effectiveness of training for interviewing (Chapter 3). 'Its survival and growth are based on faith.' One research programme on which he comments especially favourably is concerned with group training and with *when* interviewing skills are learned most successfully.

Mackenzie Davey places great emphasis on the need for other tools to back up the interview, such as personality questionnaires and psychological tests. He stresses the need for a sound understanding of personality theory and much experience in interpreting the data collected if the interview and the combined techniques that can measure certain personal characteristics are to be successful. Fletcher (Chapter 4) reinforces these views on the interview used on its own.

The judicious use of psychological tests can greatly help selectors, but for the non-psychologist professional advice, and also training, is essential before tests can be reliably used to improve the quality of judgement. Specialist guidance is needed too in the selection of appropriate tests. Little can be learned from the inspection of tests. Anyone proposing to use tests would be reckless to introduce them without making sure that they were appropriate, reliable, and valid. Statistical rather than anecdotal evidence is required. This point is underlined by Fletcher when he evaluates the work of assessment centres, where the face validity of the procedure and what it sets out to measure is 'almost frighteningly high'.

Properly used, assessment centres probably constitute one of the most effective selection/judgement tools, however. What has been done here by the British Army and by the Civil Service Selection Board is worth looking at. These boards and others, such as AT & T,[3] plus the centres described by Fletcher, are all boards composed of highly trained professionals. All used psychological tests as well as the subjective judgement procedures. Ungerson has commented[4] that 'It is quite fallacious to assume that similar validities can be achieved by programmes using non-specialists with brief training and without the contribution of pencil and paper tests.' But such techniques are really suited only to organizations doing large-scale recruitment or management development.

The less conventional techniques presented in this book appear to offer little practical help. For instance, Bayne (Chapter 10) does not suggest that at this stage selectors are likely to gain anything of great value from palmistry. If it does indeed measure personality, Bayne finds that palmistry has some special strengths. It seems to be a reliable test: trained raters should usually agree with each other, the palmist's assessment should not be influenced by the candidate's or the client's boredom, enthusiasm, suspicion, etc., and faking should not be a problem. Moreover, palmistry is not expensive. Bayne concludes that, while the evidence on palmistry as a measure of personality is by no means conclusive, the method is worth following up.

The dangers inherent in amateur graphology are acute since elementary and untrained interpretations of handwriting can be most misleading. The concept that handwriting expresses personality is an attractive one and has appealed for a long time. The Roman historian Suetonius Tranquillus, as well as Aristotle, are known to have shown interest in the subject, and there are regular references to handwriting and character over succeeding centuries. By the mid-nineteenth century serious attempts were being made, especially in France, to develop a science of the study of handwriting, and the word 'graphology' appeared at about that time. Towards the end of the nineteenth century the main interest in graphology moved from France to Germany, where it has been developed and has remained a prominent topic. Graphology has gained academic status in many universities but has still not achieved scientific recognition. There seems to be far more art than science in the interpretation of handwriting, yet the notion that the key to understanding personality could lie in this very individualistic piece of behaviour remains intriguing.

Defenders of graphology argue that handwriting should be called 'brain-writing', since its form is determined by forces within the individual. It is noticeable that people trained initially to write in the same style soon develop very personal and identifiable different forms of writing. Most of us can identify the writing of friends at a glance. Because personality is not static, writing changes throughout a person's life. Although there seems to be a powerful *a priori* case for the study of handwriting, and research into such measurable factors as size, proportion, and angles would be relatively straightforward, no simple key to interpreting these differences has in fact been found.

There may well be gifted graphologists in the same way as there are gifted intuitive judges; but, just as the gifted judge cannot teach his less sensitive associates, neither, apparently, can the gifted graphologist pass on his art. The matter is not as simple as saying that (as at least one book on graphology puts it) 'broadly based writing shows force of character', 'angular writing reflects an active mind and refinement' or, as noted elsewhere, 'angular writing means penetration and quick temper'. Loewenthal points to the many pitfalls in this field (Chapter 7). She urges us to beware of our own amateur attempts to read character from handwriting. 'Professional graphology may give better results but it is not wholly reliable; there are probably cheaper and more valid methods of personality assessment to suit most contingencies.'

Nevertheless, it is difficult totally to abandon the thought that handwriting, which is so personal and unique, does not reflect something of the make-up of the writer. The obvious unscientific test—to send copies of the handwriting of four or five friends or well-known colleagues for analysis—could be a trap. Graphologists (and not only graphologists) can write ambiguously, and the report can often play on the suggestibility of the reader. 'Yes, come to think of it, she does tend to become a little flustered under stress.' It is plainly a technique worth watching. It is not impossible that, with the aid of computers, a breakthrough could lead to the more scientific interpretation of handwriting.

Seen for years by many conventional assessors as representing one of the extremes of charlatanism, astrologists have more recently startled parts of the scientific world by producing some seemingly unshakable statistical analyses. The work done by the Gauquelins in France, and later by Eysenck and Nias in Britain, has provided evidence that the positions of planets at the moment of birth may have had an influence on the future development of an individual. But even the most devoted supporter would not claim that this is a simple matter. MacCleod, an enthusiastic and largely intuitive astrologer, points out in Chapter 8 that the simple Sun signs used in popular newspapers are grossly inadequate. There would appear to be no defensible case for simply finding out whether a candidate was a Leo or a Scorpio and basing one's predictions on the crude, generalized characteristics given to the 12 Sun signs: common sense suggests that there are far more than 12 personality types. In his complementary chapter (Chapter 9), Nias does not paint a rosy picture of astrology in general. 'But for the scientist, if there is any truth at all in astrology, then it is of the most profound importance. . . . It will be interesting to see what happens.'

Thus we conclude that a more detailed analysis of astrological charts and planetary influences must be carried out. If it emerges that we can learn something about personality from astrological data, it is unlikely to be a simple matter. On the evidence currently available, it would call for considerable analysis and interpretation.

The major trap in judging people is over-simplification. In Chapter 6, Cook quotes Hartshorne and May,[5] who, over 50 years ago, found that a trait as seemingly straightforward as 'honesty' was not consistent: children who would lie about one matter would not cheat on another. More recent experiments seem to confirm the inconsistency of apparently fundamental traits. We therefore cannot hope for simple tests of 'integrity', 'aggression', or 'attitude to authority'. The more one examines judging people, the more complex and subtle the process becomes.

For the non-professional selector, the person who is interested in what has influenced judgement in the past, what is continuing to influence judgement, and what will influence it in the future, the possibilities are fruitful and exciting. He can take time to relate the ideas of the ancients to the present-day computer-based technology, and to bring together the mystical ideas of the clairvoyant to the seemingly scientific findings of the Kirlian photographers (as we noted in the Introduction).

These chapters discuss sound, down-to-earth techniques plus a number of alternative and more controversial approaches. Our conclusion, which may be over-cautious, is that we are for the present left, for practical purposes, with the well-tried, conventional, and even old-fashioned ideas. It would have been far more dramatic if we could have said 'forget about all your elaborate assessment centres, your psychological tests, your thoughtful interviewing; the simple answer is. . . .' Sadly, as far as we have been able to discover, there is no short-cut to the judgement of people and the prediction of how they are likely to behave, unless it is to identify and use the intuitive and gifted judge. More work is badly needed on the subject of intuitive judgement, and this is an area in which we believe that research would be well repaid.

Such explorations as we have been able to make into techniques not covered here suggest that they too offer no quick or easy answers. As we have remarked, our choice of approaches to ways of judging people has been a deliberate one, confined to methods that, while experimental as well as proven, are being continually researched. It will be interesting to see how these skills develop over a period: which may have to be dismissed and which can be reliably shown to have succeeded.

References

1. Oskamp, S., 'The relationship of clinical experience and training methods to several criteria of clinical prediction', *Psychological Monographs*, vol. 76, no. 28 (whole no. 547), 1962.
2. Vernon, P. E. and Parry, J. B., *Personnel Selection in the British Forces*, University of London Press, 1949.
3. (The AT&T study) Bray, D. W. and Grant, D. L., 'The assessment center in the measurement of potential for business management', *Psychological Monographs*, vol. 80, no. 17 (whole no. 625), 1966.
4. Ungerson, B., 'Assessment centres—a review of research findings', *Personnel Review*, vol. 3, no. 3, 4–13, 1974.
5. Hartshorne, H. and May, M. A., *Studies in Deceit*, Macmillan, New York, 1928.

Index

compiled by K. G. B. Bakewell

Authors of bibliographical references have been indexed if named in the text but not otherwise. '*n*' after a page reference indicates a footnote.

Virgo, 103
Vitality-line, 133
Vocational guidance: astrological methods, 108–10

Watson, L., 132
Webster, E. C., 56
Wedderburn, A. A. I., 61
White, O., 120
Whyte, W. F., 69
Wiggins, N., 75
Williams, R., 46

Wing, A. M., 94
Wolff, C., 132, 133, 134, 135, 138
Work style, 32, 38–9
Wright, D. S., 59–60

Zodiac, signs of (*see also* Aquarius; Aries; Capricorn; Gemini; Leo; Libra; Moon; Pisces; Planets *and names of planets*; Sun; Taurus; Virgo), 99–100, 111
charts, 103, 104, 106, 111
symbols, 100